The Apple Cider Vinegar Guide: How to Lose Weight, Improve Your Skin, Alleviate Allergies and Better Your Health with Apple Cider Vinegar

by Rachel Jones

Disclaimer:

This book is for entertainment purposes. The publisher and author of this book are not responsible in any manner whatsoever for any damages arising directly or indirectly from use of the information in this book. Use this information at your own risk. The publisher and author disclaim any liabilities for damages caused by use of the information contained herein.

None of the claims in this book should be construed as medical advice. Consult with a medical professional prior to making any changes in your life that could impact your health.

Contents

Introduction to Apple Cider Vinegar

Apple cider vinegar, affectionately known as ACV to its loyal followers, is much, much more than just a condiment or your run of the mill vinegar. Yes, it can be used in a variety of food dishes, but that isn't all it's good for. There are a number of health, fitness and household applications for apple cider vinegar.

Do a bit of research into ACV and you'll find all sorts of lofty claims made in books and on the Internet regarding it's miraculous. Some would have you believe apple cider vinegar is the only supplement you're ever going to need.

The reality is some of this information is overstated. Apple cider vinegar isn't a miracle cure-all potion capable of curing any and every ailment you may be suffering, but it does have applications in which it excels. For example, it's been shown in scientific studies to lower blood glucose and long-term consumption of apple cider vinegar has been shown to aid with moderate weight loss.

Apple cider vinegar isn't just a dietary supplement. It can also be used in the home as a natural cleaner, deodorizer and sanitizer. Replacing harsh synthetic household cleaners with all-natural apple cider vinegar is the smart choice, and it's one that could pay dividends in improved quality of life for you and your family for years down the road. Making the switch to apple cider vinegar also helps your pocketbook, as it's significantly less expensive than most commercial cleaning products.

It might surprise you to hear apple cider vinegar can also be used as a beauty product. It's believed to be good for both the skin and the hair and can be used in place of commercial products containing harsh chemicals and synthetic additives.

Since apple cider vinegar is made from nothing more than apples and water, it's completely natural. There are no toxic fumes, no harsh chemical additives and, for most people, there's little to be concerned with regarding the use of apple cider vinegar. It's generally considered safe for use in small amounts, but be sure to consult with your doctor or dietician before adding it to your diet. There may be health concerns or potential interactions with medications you aren't aware of.

A Brief History of Apple Cider Vinegar

Vinegar occurs naturally as part of the fermentation process of fruit, so it's safe to assume the discovery of vinegar predates recorded history.

Fermented fruit becomes wine, which is known to have been in use for thousands of years and was likely discovered long before that. Introduce oxygen to wine and allow it to ferment for a longer period of time than you normally would and you end up with vinegar. Wine has historically been made from a variety of fruits, one of which is apples, so there's no telling when apple cider vinegar was first discovered. It was probably discovered by accident when apple wine was left to ferment for too long.

The first recorded use of vinegar dates back to 5,000 BC, when the ancient Babylonians fermented the fruit of the date palm to make both vinegar and wine. They consumed it as a dietary staple and used it as a preservation agent for a number of food items.

Apple cider vinegar was created as a byproduct of soured apple wine.

An ancient nomadic tribe known as the Aryans are said to have developed sour apple wine, which at some point led to the production of apple cider vinegar. The Aryans at passed this knowledge on the Greeks and Romans, who began intentionally developing apple cider vinegar as a byproduct of sour apple wine.

Vinegar was used as both a food staple and a medicine. It's healing powers were legendary, and it soon spread across the globe. The Roman army consumed it, as did most Europeans. In 400 BC, Hippocrates used a combination of honey and vinegar to treat a number of illnesses and ailments. The ancient Chinese and Japanese enjoyed vinegar. Samurais are said to have drank it for its tonic qualities.

Christopher Columbus brought apple cider vinegar with him when he traveled the seas in the late 1400's, using it to fight off scurvy.

The first American settlers brought apple seeds with them and grew apples which they fermented into apple cider and apple cider vinegar. It was consumed by everyone from the average citizen to U.S. Presidents. Vinegar was used to fight scurvy during the American Civil War and saw use as a disinfectant during World War I, when it was used to treat wounds in the field prior to dressing them.

Apple cider vinegar fell out of favor at the beginning of the last century, as modern medicines rapidly replaced natural solutions and folk medicine. People were led to believe modern medicine was much more effective than traditional remedies, so the traditional remedies fell from favor.

It didn't regain popularity until Dr. D.C. Jarvis released the book *Folk Medicine: A Vermont Doctor's Guide to Good Health* in 1958. Apple cider vinegar moved back into the limelight when Dr. Jarvis made the claim two teaspoons of vinegar mixed with two teaspoons of honey mixed in a glass of water could cure a number of illnesses and ailments (1).

Fast forward to modern times and we're just now realizing the many benefits of apple cider vinegar. It's quickly becoming apparent our ancestors may have been onto something when they used apple cider vinegar to improve their health.

What is Apple Cider Vinegar?

Apple cider vinegar, in its purest form, is a strongly acidic compound made by crushing organic apples and allowing them to ferment until they turn into vinegar. During the fermentation process, yeasts and bacteria already present on the skins of the apples go to work. The first stage of fermentation sees the sugars in the apples converted into alcohol. If fermentation is stopped at this point, sour apple wine is the result. If left to ferment further, the alcohol in the wine is converted to acid and apple cider vinegar is created.

Acetic acid bacteria are the bacteria responsible for creating most of the acid in apple cider vinegar. These bacteria require oxygen to thrive, so apple cider vinegar is typically fermented in a container into which air can circulate. Wine and hard ciders, on the other hand, are fermented in airtight containers in order to create an environment that isn't conducive to growth of acetic acid bacteria.

As acetic acid bacteria transform alcohol into acetic acid, the alcohol content of the apple cider drops and the acidity increases. How strong the finished vinegar will be is determined by how much alcohol there is in the cider. More alcohol equates to more acidic vinegar.

In addition to acetic acid, there are more than 90 different compounds known to exist in apple cider vinegar. Every time vinegar is fermented, the composition of the final product is different. The chemical composition of the vinegar depends on a number of external factors. No wonder scientists are having trouble pinning down the true health value of apple cider vinegar.

The Mother of Bacteria

Pure apple cider vinegar is dark and cloudy and contains a fibrous substance called **mother of bacteria**, or simply "the mother." The mother is made up of cellulose and acetic acid bacteria. Vinegars containing the mother contain beneficial bacteria and enzymes the filtered vinegars don't have.

Whenever you see apple cider vinegar referred to in this book, it's vinegar with the mother in it that's being referenced. Vinegar with the mother in it has more health value than vinegar with the mother filtered out. The clear vinegars you see on store shelves have been processed and refined to remove the mother of vinegar.

Nutritional Information for ACV

Before we go any further, let's take a quick look at the nutritional information for apple cider vinegar.

A couple tablespoons of ACV taken daily will only add 5 to 6 calories to your diet. People typically spread the consumption out across the day, adding a couple teaspoons of apple cider vinegar to a glass of water and drinking it 1 to 2 times a day. Apple cider vinegar doesn't contain any fat and measures 0 on the glycemic index, so a tablespoon a day will have a relatively small impact on most diets.

Acetic acid is the main compound found in apple cider vinegar. Many of the health benefits associated with vinegar are attributed to the acetic acid, but scientists don't fully understand why. More studies are needed to make the connection between acetic acid and the many health benefits it's thought to have.

There are a number of beneficial compounds found in ACV, including the following:

- Acetic acid.
- Amino acids.
- Calcium.
- Carbolic acids.
- Copper.
- Fluorine.
- Iron.
- Ketones.
- Magnesium.

- Phosphorous.
- Potassium.
- Sulfur.

Apple cider vinegar with the mother in it contains these compounds and then some. Don't attempt to use apple cider vinegar without the mother in it because many of these nutrients will have been processed out of it.

How to Make Apple Cider Vinegar

Let me preface this chapter by stating you don't have to make your own apple cider vinegar, as it's relatively inexpensive to purchase. You can get an entire gallon of organic unfiltered apple cider vinegar for around $20 on Amazon. If you're like most people, a gallon should last you quite some time.

If you want to save a little money and have some fun, apple cider vinegar can be fermented at home.

In order to make apple cider vinegar, first you're going to need apple cider. You can purchase apple cider, but it's probably going to cost you more for the apple cider than it would to just buy apple cider vinegar. The less-expensive option is to gather a bunch of apples and make them into apple cider yourself.

The best apples for apple cider vinegar are sweeter red apples because they have high sugar content. Sour green apples don't work well because they don't have as much sugar that can be fermented in alcohol.

Follow these steps to make apple cider vinegar:

1. **Gather apples.** Sweet apples are the best choice for apple cider vinegar. Use organic apples to avoid the pesticides and other chemicals that are sprayed on conventionally grown apples.
2. **Wash the apples.** Give them a good rub down to rid them of debris.
3. **Juice the apples by crushing them and straining the juice through a filter or**

cheesecloth. Strain the apple juice a couple times to get rid of most of the debris floating in the juice.

4. **Gather the container(s) in which you plan to ferment the vinegar.** I prefer glass containers because they're nonreactive. Steer clear of metal containers because they can react with the acids in the vinegar and can leach unwanted compounds into the vinegar.

5. **Pour the apple cider into the container(s).**

6. **Add yeast or unfiltered apple cider vinegar to the container.** This step is optional, but will get your apple cider vinegar off to a quicker start. Not adding yeast or ACV will result in longer fermentation times. You can add a bit of apple cider vinegar that contains mother of vinegar in it or, if you don't have unfiltered apple cider vinegar on hand, wine-making shops should carry the cultures you need.

7. **Place a cloth lid on the container.** Don't cap the container tightly. Vinegar won't form without oxygen being present in the container. Cover the container with cheesecloth and tie or rubber band it in place. This will keep bugs out while allowing air to circulate into the container.

8. **Place the container in an area of the house with an ambient temperature around 70° F.** Keep the container out of bright light and away from heat sources, as exposure to either of these items can damage the acetic acid bacteria that ferment the vinegar.

9. **Let the container sit for a month (or longer).**
   It'll start to smell like alcohol and will then start
   smelling like vinegar. After a month, sample the
   vinegar frequently and bottle it once it reaches
   the desired strength.

Keep in mind the ACV will continue fermenting after
you bottle it if you leave the mother of vinegar in it. You
can filter most of the mother of vinegar out of the ACV by
filtering it through cheesecloth. This will slow fermentation
and prolong the life of the cider, but will also eliminate
some of the probiotic bacteria in the vinegar.

Ideally, apple cider vinegar should be 4% to 6% acid.
It's tough to control how acidic vinegar is when making it
at home, so don't use homemade apple cider vinegar for
tasks like pickling foods where the acid content is critical to
safety. There are test kits available that you can use to
check the acidity of your cider, but you're still better off
using commercial vinegars for pickling purposes. When
you consider the risks are botulism and other types of food
poisoning, the stakes are too high to take chances.

Buying Apple Cider Vinegar

If you'd rather purchase apple cider vinegar from the store, it's easy. There's only one type of vinegar you should buy. Organic, unfiltered, unpasteurized apple cider vinegar is the only ACV you should buy. Here's why.

Organic apple cider vinegar is crafted from organic apples, which are apples grown naturally, without use of harsh chemical pesticides, herbicides and fertilizers. The chemicals sprayed on conventionally-grown apples make it into the apples themselves and trace amounts of these chemicals can end up in vinegar made from them. These chemicals build up in your system over time and can cause a number of health problems later on down the road. Eating foods made from organic produce are a good choice because they eliminate a lot of chemicals from your diet.

Most people balk at buying organic food because of the cost difference. Organic foods usually cost significantly more than non-organic foods, but this simply isn't the case with apple cider vinegar. Non-organic apple cider vinegar may be available, but the cost difference isn't enough to be of concern, especially when you consider the potential long-term impact on your health.

Filtered vinegar is the most common type of vinegar on store shelves. Filtered ACV is light to golden brown in color and is usually crystal clear. This is because the mother of vinegar and much of the beneficial flora have been filtered out of the vinegar. People who don't know what they're missing out on won't buy cloudy vinegar and prefer the clear, clean-looking stuff.

Those in the know prefer the unfiltered, cloudy stuff because they know it contains the mother of vinegar. Remove the mother and you remove a lot of the health value of vinegar.

The last item to look at when buying ACV is to make sure it hasn't been pasteurized. The pasteurization process kills off all of the bacteria in the vinegar. The heat used during pasteurization also damages some of the vitamins and nutrients found in the vinegar. It's done to keep the vinegar from continuing to ferment on store shelves, but the reality is it kills much of the health value.

The following brands of apple cider vinegar all meet the requirements outlined in this chapter:

- Bragg Organic Raw Apple Cider Vinegar.
- Fleischmann's Organic Apple Cider Vinegar.
- Dynamic Health Organic Apple Cider Vinegar.
- Eden Organic Apple Cider Vinegar.
- Spectrum Naturals Organic Apple Cider Vinegar.
- Vitacost Organic Apple Cider Vinegar.

Keep in mind this list isn't all-inclusive. If you look inside the bottle and it's cloudy and there's mother of vinegar floating inside, that's a good sign you're on the right track.

I use Bragg Organic Apple Cider Vinegar myself because it's one of the oldest and most trusted brands. It's also available at the grocery store in the small town I live in, which makes it easy to source.

Possible Side Effects

Before we get into the use of apple cider vinegar, it's important to discuss the potential side effects of consuming too much of this potent elixir. While there are a number of health benefits thought to be associated with apple cider vinegar, it isn't a completely benign compound. There are some side effects you need to be aware of.

One of the biggest problems associated with apple cider vinegar is its potential to damage your teeth.

The acids in the vinegar can permanently erode tooth enamel, which can lead to decay and badly damaged teeth. This problem is more pronounced in those who take it straight as opposed to diluting it with water. Always dilute ACV in a cup of water and rinse out your mouth after taking it. Drinking diluted apple cider vinegar with a straw will help keep it away from your teeth. Wait a half hour to brush your teeth, as the compounds in toothpaste may react with the acids in the vinegar, causing further damage to your teeth.

There are people who recommend taking a teaspoon or two of apple cider vinegar straight a couple times a day instead of diluting it. This is a bad idea because it's more damaging to the teeth at full strength and the acids in the ACV can burn the soft tissues of the mouth and throat.

Another concern with apple cider vinegar is the potential for interaction with prescription medications. ACV is said to interact negatively with diuretics, heart disease medications and some diabetes drugs. You should always consult with your doctor prior to adding ACV to your diet, but it's especially important if you're currently taking prescription medications. You don't want to make current health conditions worse by taking apple cider vinegar. Of particular concern are drugs that deplete potassium in the body. Since apple cider vinegar can also deplete potassium, the potential exists for the body to run low on potassium.

Adding ACV to Your Diet

For most people, the worst thing about apple cider vinegar is the taste. Taste is the number one biggest complaint amongst people who take it as a supplement.

The most commonly recommended method of taking ACV doesn't do much to get rid of the taste. Most people mix a tablespoon or two of ACV into a cup of water and pound it down. While water dilutes apple cider vinegar enough to where it probably isn't going to burn your mouth or throat, you're still painfully aware you're drinking vinegar. I don't know what's worse—the taste while it's going down or the aftertaste you get moments after you chug it.

Some people recommend adding honey to make it more tolerable. This works, but you still get the strong aftertaste of vinegar.

Adding ACV to fruit juices like orange juice or apple juice can also help the vinegar go down smoother. You'll still get the slight aftertaste of vinegar, but it's nowhere near as bad as it tastes without the juice. Some people recommend adding it to smoothies, but I don't really like the idea of drinking an entire smoothie that has the aftertaste of vinegar.

Another method of adding it to your diet is to combine your daily serving of ACV with virgin olive oil and drizzle it over a salad. There's something to be said about the way the flavors of oil and vinegar meld with tasty greens in a leafy salad.

Apple cider vinegar supplements are available in pill form, but these supplements aren't regulated and it isn't clear what is and isn't included in them. You aren't likely to get the same good stuff you get from unfiltered ACV if you take it in pill form.

Health Benefits of Apple Cider Vinegar

There are a handful of scientifically proven health benefits of apple cider vinegar and a much larger number of benefits that haven't been given proper attention by the scientific community. Studies of the benefits of apple cider vinegar are sorely lacking, probably because there isn't much money to be made by proving apple cider vinegar works as an effective home remedy for ailments and illnesses. There aren't many companies willing to fund studies that prove their medications aren't necessary.

There's still a lot to be learned about apple cider vinegar. To date, there are only 22 studies that pop up when you search "apple cider vinegar" on PubMed.gov, which is a database of peer reviewed scientific studies. This is surprising when you consider the vast number of health claims made about ACV. In contrast, searching "coconut oil," in the same database reveals 1475 studies.

This chapter discusses both documented health benefits that are backed up by scientific studies and the uses for apple cider vinegar that people swear by, but haven't yet been proven or disproven in a laboratory setting.

Allergies

When springtime rolls around and plants start releasing clouds of pollen into the air, millions of Americans are struck with seasonal allergies. It's estimated that 1 in 5 people suffer from some form of allergy. While hay fever is usually seasonal, some people suffer from allergies year-round, regardless of the season.

Allergies occur when the body senses a foreign substance and reacts to it with an inappropriately strong immune system response. The foreign substance is harmless, but the body doesn't see it that way. It sees it as a threat and tries to dispel it. This is where the coughing, mucous, stuffy head, runny nose and other symptoms come from. They're the way the body attempts to get rid of the substance.

People can be allergic to a number of things, including the following:

- **Dust.**
- **Food.**
- **Mold.**
- **Pets.**
- **Pollen.**

The symptoms of an allergy attack can range from mild to severe, with most sufferers experiencing stuffy heads, itchy eyes and running noses. Some people suffer from the beginning of the day to the end, and gain little to no relief from modern medications.

The following symptoms are some of the more common symptoms of allergies:

- **Bloody nose.**
- **Cough.**
- **Headache.**
- **Itchy and/or runny nose.**
- **Itchy, dry or sore throat.**
- **Itchy skin.**
- **Nasal congestion.**
- **Rash.**
- **Red and itchy eyes.**
- **Sneezing.**

Sufferers of seasonal allergies may want to give apple cider vinegar a try to see if it provides relief. There haven't been any major studies supporting use of apple cider vinegar for allergy relief, but that doesn't necessarily mean it doesn't work. It just means no team of scientists has studied it to either prove or disprove its effectiveness.

What we do know is there are a lot of users of apple cider vinegar who claim it reduces their allergy symptoms. The sneezing, stuffy head and itchy and watery eyes don't always go away, but they can be made more tolerable. When you consider that allergy medications are expensive and can be ineffective for some people, you may be able to get the same effect or better from apple cider vinegar for pennies on the dollar.

There's no guarantee it'll work, but it's worth a shot.

Try a tablespoon of apple cider vinegar mixed into a cup of water daily if you're suffering from allergies.

Alternatively, mix the following ingredients together to make an allergy tonic:

- **1 cup water.**
- **1 tablespoon apple cider vinegar.**
- **1 tablespoon raw honey.**
- **2 tablespoons lemon juice.**

It may take a week or two before you see any results.

Never attempt to use apple cider vinegar to treat a serious allergic reaction. If you're suffering severe symptoms like swelling, difficulty breathing or shortness of breath, seek immediate medical attention. A severe allergic reaction can end in anaphylactic shock and can be fatal. You aren't going to stop this sort of allergic reaction with ACV.

Be aware that, as is the case with any food, there is a small percentage of the population that is allergic to apple cider vinegar. If you experience an allergic reaction, discontinue use and seek immediate medical attention.

Eliminate Bad Breath

A common cause of bad breath, also known as **halitosis**, is the build-up of nasty bacteria in the mouth. The bacteria that cause halitosis typically build up on the back of the tongue and around the teeth and the effect is cumulative. The longer the bacteria are allowed to grow unchecked, the worse your breath will be. Halitosis can also come about as a symptom of certain medical conditions, foods that have been consumed in the recent past and dental health concerns. It's an embarrassing problem that can negatively impact the lives of sufferers and may affect their quality of life.

Drinking a tablespoon of apple cider vinegar mixed into a cup of water *before* each meal will aid in digestion and may help eliminate bad breath. Gargling with a solution made by mixing two tablespoons of ACV into a cup of water *after* meals may also provide relief by eliminating the bacteria from the back of the tongue and the mouth. Be sure to rinse out your mouth really good because the acid in the vinegar can damage the enamel on your teeth. Wait at least a half

For additional relief, try dipping a mint sprig in vinegar and then chewing it up and swallowing it. The mint will kill harmful bacteria in the mouth and will aid with digestion when it reaches the stomach.

Balance Your Body's pH

Internal pH is a topic of much debate. On one side you have the naysayers who claim you can't change the pH of your body by making dietary changes. On the other there are a number of alternative health experts who make a pretty convincing argument that maintaining the proper pH balance in the body is the key to staying in good health. They say the human body functions best when it's slightly alkaline, but the foods we eat are acidic and the body is in a constant battle to regulate the acid created by the high volume of acid-producing foods we're eating.

The **internal pH balance** is a measurement of how acidic the blood and other bodily fluids are. The pH scale measures acidity (or lack thereof) on a scale ranging from 0 to 14. A measurement of 7 is considered neutral pH. Anything below 7 is considered acidic and can result in poor health. Measurements above 7 indicate a lack of hydrogen in the blood and are known as alkaline measurements. The ideal range for human blood is between 7.35 and 7.45 on the pH scale.

Processes like calorie burning, cell building and even breathing all create acid that can lower the pH of the blood. Stress can also create excess acid in the blood. Diet plays a huge role in alkalinity, as some foods are acidic by nature, while others create alkalinity once inside the body. The typical Western diet is much higher in acidic foods than it should be, which leads to the blood being too acidic.

This is problematic because the body tries to rid itself of extra acid at the expense of minerals stored in the bones, teeth and tissues of the body. The main mineral used by the body to control acid is calcium, but there are a number of other minerals used as well. It's important these minerals are replaced or health problems related to the mineral loss will crop up.

Once the mineral supply runs low, the body starts attacking the acids in the blood in a more destructive manner. It can lock the excess acid away in fat cells that are hard to get rid of and in muscle tissue. An immune system response due to the body being unable to cope with the acids in the blood can result and all sorts of health problems can manifest as a result. When the body drops into the acidic pH range and stays there, **acidosis** can occur. Arthritis, strokes, heart disease and cancer are just a handful of the many problems thought to be associated with too much acid in the body.

To properly balance the acids being produced and consumed, you have to consume a higher volume of foods that are alkalizing than foods that are acidic. Foods like white bread, processed foods, alcohol and foods that are high in sugar are all strongly acidic. Meats and fish, legumes, grains, nuts and dairy products are mildly acidic. Most fruits and vegetables are alkalizing and eating more of them will help get your system back on track.

To further muddle the issue, the actual acid content of a food has little bearing on whether or not it forms acids in the body. Even though apple cider vinegar contains large amounts of acetic acid and a number of other acids, it has an alkalizing effect on the human body once consumed. Regular consumption of apple cider vinegar can help rebalance the body toward the desired alkalinity. There's no standard recommended dosage, but most people take between 1 teaspoon and 2 tablespoons of vinegar mixed with a cup of water per day.

Drinking a couple tablespoons of ACV mixed with water a day won't eliminate the acidic effects of a bad diet, so don't assume consuming apple cider vinegar will allow you to make poor diet choices. On the other hand, ACV coupled with a diet of 60% alkalizing foods and 40% acidic foods could be the difference between being healthy and developing serious health problems later on down the road.

Blood Pressure, Cholesterol and Heart Disease

Thousands of Americans die daily due to some form of cardiovascular disease. According to the Center for Disease Control and Prevention (CDC), heart disease is the leading cause of death for both men and women. Approximately 600,000 people die every year from heart disease.

High blood pressure and high LDL cholesterol are both key risk factors for heart disease. Preliminary studies have shown apple cider vinegar or the compounds found in apple cider vinegar may be able to help with both high blood pressure and LDL cholesterol levels.

The next 2 sections discuss apple cider vinegar and its effect on blood pressure and cholesterol. These areas are some of the most heavily studied uses for apple cider vinegar in the scientific community. The preliminary studies have largely shown good results and more research is warranted.

Blood Pressure

Blood pressure, also known as arterial blood pressure, is the pressure blood exerts on the walls of blood vessels as it circulates through the body. Blood pressure is measured by taking both a systolic and diastolic reading. As the heart pumps blood through the body the pressure waxes and wanes with each beat of the heart. **Systolic pressure** is the maximum arterial pressure placed on the veins, while the **diastolic pressure** is the minimum arterial pressure.

Blood pressure is measured by measuring the pressure in the brachial artery in the upper arm, which is one of the main arteries coming from the heart. The desired systolic blood pressure in the average adult is between 90 and 120 and the desired diastolic pressure is between 60 and 80. Those with high blood pressure are said to be suffering various stages of **hypertension**.

The following chart shows the various stages of hypertension:

Stage	Systolic (mm Hg)	Diastolic (mm Hg)
Normal	80 to 120	60 to 80
Prehypertension	120 to 139	80 to 89
Stage 1 Hypertension	140 to 159	90 to 99
Stage 2 Hypertension	160 or above	100 or above
Emergency	180 or above	110 or above

Blood pressure can go up and down throughout the day and may change over time. Stress, obesity, smoking, lack of exercise, diet and genetics are just some of the factors that can affect blood pressure. If a doctor suspects you have high blood pressure, the doctor may want to have you take periodic blood pressure tests over a longer timeframe to see if the current reading is an anomaly or the norm.

Consistently high readings are problematic because the heart has to work harder to pump blood throughout the body than it should. Hypertension can lead to heart problems, hardened arteries and an increased risk of heart failure.

When it comes to using apple cider vinegar to help lower blood pressure there is quite a bit of anecdotal evidence backed up by a handful of studies. The preliminary studies done thus far are promising, plus there are large numbers of people on various sites across the Internet claiming to have lowered their blood pressure by consuming apple cider vinegar. Take it for what it's worth, but there may actually be something to it.

A 2006 study done by the Central Research Institute at Kyoto University in Japan showed long-term administration of acetic acid or vinegar to rats resulted in a significant reduction in blood pressure in comparison to rats fed the same diet without vinegar (2). Vinegar was shown to be slightly more effective than acetic acid alone. Whether or not this equates to a similar drop in blood pressure in humans who consume ACV remains to be seen.

The second study was done using **querticin**, which is an antioxidant flavonol found in apples. This study looked at

41 men and women with prehypertension or stage 1 hypertension and showed querticin to be effective in lowering blood pressure (3). While this study showed promising results, it isn't clear whether there's enough querticin in apple cider vinegar to make a difference.

To my knowledge, there have been no studies done on humans to investigate the connection between apple cider vinegar and its ability to lower blood pressure. Based on the results of the aforementioned studies, a closer look at ACV and its relationship to blood pressure is warranted, especially in light of all the anecdotal evidence in its favor.

As far as taking apple cider vinegar to help with blood pressure, there's no medically recommended amount because it hasn't been studied. It's probably best to start with a teaspoon or less a day in a glass of water and work your way up to a tablespoon or two daily. As with any new dietary addition, discuss adding apple cider vinegar to your diet with your doctor prior to actually adding it.

This is especially important if you're currently taking prescription medications for high blood pressure.

Apple cider vinegar is said to interact negatively with diuretics, which are a type of medicine commonly prescribed to people with high blood pressure. Diuretics decrease the level of potassium in the body. Apple cider vinegar is known to also decrease potassium, so combining the two could result in depleted potassium reserves in the body. Potassium deficiency is known as hypokalemia in the medical world and can carry serious consequences. It can make your already high blood pressure even higher and chronic potassium shortage ups the long-term risk for osteoporosis. Potassium deficiencies can also result in muscle damage and, in serious cases, paralysis, kidney failure and heart problems can occur.

Cholesterol

Cholesterol is the second part of the heart disease double-whammy. It's also one of the most misunderstood compounds in the human body. People hear the word cholesterol and instantly start thinking bad thoughts, but the reality is your body needs a small amount of cholesterol to function.

Cholesterol is a fat-like substance found in pretty much every cell in the human body. It's used in a number of bodily functions.

Lipoproteins carry cholesterol through your blood stream. These carriers, made of fat and protein, wrap themselves around cholesterol molecules and transport them throughout the body. There are two basic types of lipoproteins: **low-density lipoproteins (LDL)** and **high-density lipoproteins (HDL)**. LDL cholesterol is said to be bad cholesterol because it deposits itself on the walls of arteries as it travels through the bloodstream. White blood cells attempt to get rid of the LDL cholesterol and inflammation occurs in the area of the deposit. Over time, a substance called **plaque** forms in the arteries as cholesterol and white blood cells collect and gather debris. Plaque is dangerous because it can gather to the point it blocks arteries. It can also rupture and cause a heart attack.

HDL cholesterol is known as good cholesterol because HDL molecules transport excess cholesterol out of the body via the liver. These molecules don't gather on artery walls the way LDL cholesterol does.

People who are said to suffer from high cholesterol have elevated levels of LDL cholesterol. Having high LDL cholesterol puts you at increased risk of heart disease because it can cause excess plaque build-up both in the heart and the arteries.

HDL cholesterol isn't a deciding factor when it comes to high cholesterol because having high HDL cholesterol isn't problematic. People with higher HDL cholesterol are at *less risk* of heart disease because their system is more likely to clear out excess cholesterol.

Diet is the main source of excess cholesterol in the body. Any food that comes from an animal contains cholesterol, so go easy on the animal products. Lean cuts of meat have as much or more cholesterol than the fatty cuts, so don't think you can avoid cholesterol by trimming off the fat. Those with high levels of cholesterol may benefit from a vegan diet or at least one that goes easy on the meat.

The typical Western diet includes large amounts of bad cholesterol. The problem with dietary cholesterol lies in the fact that your body already makes all of the cholesterol it needs. Adding too much cholesterol via your diet can result in dangerous levels of LDL cholesterol.

Apple cider vinegar is thought to help lower cholesterol. There is quite a bit of anecdotal evidence supporting this theory backed up by a select few studies.

In a paper published in the British Journal of Nutrition, scientists found that rats fed a diet containing cholesterol and acetic acid, the main component in vinegar, had decreased serum cholesterol and triglycerides in comparison to rats fed a diet of just cholesterol (4). In a recent Iranian study, scientists found apple cider vinegar reduced LDL cholesterol and increased HDL cholesterol in both normal and diabetic rats (5).

An earlier study on women who consumed oil and vinegar salad dressing at least 5 times a week revealed they were 50% less likely to die from heart attack when compared to women who didn't consume oil and vinegar dressing regularly (6). Interestingly enough, this study was commissioned to study the effect of oil-based dressings containing alpha-linoleic acid and doesn't mention the acetic acid in the vinegar as a possible reason for the reduction in heart disease. The reduction in heart attacks could have been due to the vinegar, the oil or a synergetic effect created by combining both the oil and the vinegar and consuming it daily.

It would be interesting to see a study that eliminates the oil and looks at just vinegar as salad dressing. It would also be interesting to see further scientific studies done on humans and the effect vinegar consumption has on cholesterol.

Apple cider vinegar may be able to help lower bad cholesterol, but there haven't been enough studies to prove it an effective treatment. If you'd like to try it, discuss it with your doctor to see if it's a viable option. Combined with a regular exercise and a healthy diet, it might be a lifesaver.

Cancer Prevention

The preliminary research into the ability of apple cider vinegar to prevent cancer cells from forming in the body has been positive. There have been very few studies to date, but the ones that have been done have shown vinegar to have antitumor properties.

A 2004 study published in *Biofactors* found naturally fermented sugar cane vinegar to induce apoptosis in leukemia cells (7). **Apoptosis**, also known as **programmed cell death**, occurs when a cell sends out signals letting surrounding cells know it's ready to die. The cell dies and is vacuumed up by little cleaners called **macrophages** whose job is to clear the cell out of the body. Keep in mind this study was done on different types of vinegar than apple cider vinegar, but the study did look at other naturally fermented vinegars that have radical-scavenging activity.

In 2011, Japanese researchers tested the effects of feeding the sediment from the bottom of jars of fermented rice vinegar to rats with carcinomas and found rats fed a diet containing the sediment had smaller tumors and lived longer than the rats in the control group (8). A previous experiment proved the sediment worked against colon cancer cells implanted into rats (9). The sediment used in the experiment didn't contain acetic acid, so it had to be one of the other compounds in the vinegar that affected the cells.

The exact compounds in vinegar that have the antitumor effects haven't yet been identified, but there are a number of theories. Acetic acid has been shown in a number of animal studies to have antitumor effects, but the fact that it wasn't present in the sediment is puzzling. Vinegar also contains polyphenols and a number of other antioxidant compounds that may aid with cancer prevention (10).

A study done in Linzhou City in China, where oesophageal cancer rates have rocketed sky-high in recent years, examined more than 800 people in an attempt to gain an understanding of the risk factors that contributed to the high number of citizens with cancer. The consumption of vinegar decreased the odds of developing esophageal cancer in those who consumed it (11).

It isn't known whether vinegar has the same anti-cancer effects on other types of cancer or whether apple cider vinegar is as effective as the types of vinegars used in the experiments. Because of this, there is no recommended dosage of ACV to help the body ward off cancer.

Cold Relief

The next time you find yourself coughing, sniffling and sneezing due to a cold, instead of turning to over-the-counter medications like cough syrups and antihistamines, you might want to consider apple cider vinegar instead. It's said to be an effective folk remedy for the cold and for many of the symptoms associated with the cold. ACV is said to help ease sore throats, congestion and coughs, all of which commonly present themselves as cold symptoms.

ACV acts on the common cold on multiple levels.

It helps rebalance the pH of the body, which may be in an acidic state because of the cold (12). This rebalancing may shorten the duration of a cold you're suffering and keeping your body alkaline could help it ward off future colds. Apple cider vinegar can also help thin mucus and make the cold more tolerable. The acids in the vinegar will help to neutralize any germs in the mouth and in the throat on the way down.

Apple cider vinegar alone can be mixed with water and consumed to help ease the symptoms of the common cold or you can add a couple items to the mix to make it even more effective. Here's a quick and easy cold remedy recipe you can whip up in no time at the first sign of a cold:

- **1 cup water.**
- **2 tablespoons apple cider vinegar.**
- **2 tablespoons raw honey.**
- **1 tablespoon fresh lemon juice.**
- **1 teaspoon cayenne pepper.**

The honey will help soothe your throat and may help ease symptoms of the cold. The cayenne pepper is a natural anti-inflammatory that can help reduce fevers and relieve congestion. Lemon is thought to decrease the strength of the cold and it contains vitamin C the body needs for immunity.

Detoxify the Body

The world is full of harmful compounds. They're in the air we breathe, the water we drink and the food we eat. Over time, these contaminants build up in the body and can eventually start to cause serious medical conditions. It's important to cleanse the body of contaminants from time to time.

Apple cider vinegar is a popular solution people turn to when they want to detox their system. There's even a diet called the **apple cider detox diet** that some people use. This diet calls for consuming 1 to 3 teaspoons of apple cider vinegar 15 minutes before each meal in order to help the body digest the meal and to eliminate toxins from the body.

Apple cider vinegar is believed to destroy free radicals in the body, while helping the kidneys and liver detoxify the body (13). It's antibacterial and antifungal by nature, so it theoretically should help clean harmful bacteria and fungus out of your system.

Try mixing a teaspoon or two of vinegar into a glass of water and drinking it a couple times a day. The best time to consume apple cider vinegar is just before mealtime, so it wouldn't be a bad idea to drink one cup before breakfast and one before dinner.

Diabetes

Let me begin this chapter by definitively stating there hasn't been enough research done into apple cider vinegar and diabetes to make any solid conclusions regarding its effectiveness at treating or preventing this deadly disease. The few studies that have been done have shown promising results and the preliminary evidence indicates apple cider vinegar may be a healthy choice for both diabetics and prediabetics, but more research needs to be done before any conclusions can be drawn.

Do not attempt to regulate your blood sugar using apple cider vinegar at this time. If you have diabetes and are interested in natural solutions, discuss your options with a dietician, as well as your doctor. There may be dietary changes you can make to help regulate your blood sugar.

The handful of studies done thus far appear to indicate vinegar dampens the rise in blood sugar levels normally seen after eating and may be able to help control both blood sugar and insulin. Perhaps the most revealing of the testing done thus far regarding vinegar's interaction with blood glucose and insulin levels is the research by Carol S. Johnston at Arizona State University.

The first study, published in the scientific journal *Diabetes Care* in 2004, tested both nondiabetic and diabetic subjects with type 2 diabetes. Subjects wore given a solution with apple cider vinegar in it or a placebo and then consumed a meal that consisted of a bagel, butter and orange juice. Blood samples were taken at the beginning of the test, at 30 minutes after eating the meal and at 60 minutes after the meal. Vinegar consumption lowered both the insulin response and the glucose levels found in the blood in both diabetic and nondiabetic patients. The difference was most pronounced in patients who were insulin resistant, but hadn't yet become diabetic (14).

An August 2007 study by Johnson published in *Diabetes Care* found that vinegar ingestion at bedtime favorably impacted glucose concentrations upon waking in patients with type 2 diabetes who weren't taking insulin. The test group was relatively small at only 11 subjects, but the results were promising. Participants who ate just cheese and water prior to bedtime had a 2% reduction in fasting glucose, while the subjects who consumed 2 tablespoons of apple cider vinegar with the cheese and wine saw a 4% decrease (15).

This experiment appears to confirm research done in 1987 at Ehime University in Japan. Scientists there first tested lab rats and found the rapid spike in blood glucose that usually comes after eating was diminished in lab rats given acetic acid via a stomach tube in comparison to those who weren't administered acetic acid. The next set of tests were run on two groups of healthy humans who were administered a sucrose solution. One group was given vinegar with the sucrose, while the other wasn't. The group given the vinegar with the sucrose had a lower serum insulin response (16).

A third study by the Arizona State team led by Carol Johnston was published in January of 2010. Participants in this study ate a bagel, butter and fruit juice with or without vinegar. This study revealed that taking two teaspoons of vinegar at mealtime was more effective than taking the vinegar 5 hours before the meal. It was also shown that vinegar was effective when consumed with complex carbohydrates, but didn't have the same effect when consumed with simple sugars (17). This appears to indicate vinegar somehow slows the digestive process because it works on carbohydrates that have to be broken down during digestion, but not on simple sugars are already broken down.

The most recent study from the Arizona State University team was published in April 2013 in *The FASEB Journal*. This study looked at the effect of daily vinegar consumption on both healthy and prediabetic participants. The participants were separated into two groups. The first group was given a drink containing 1 tablespoon of apple cider vinegar, while the other group was given 1 vinegar pill, which are available as dietary supplements, prior to both their lunch and dinner meals. Glucose levels were tested twice daily for 12 weeks. The tests were administered in the mornings when the patients woke up in a fasted state and again a couple hours after eating. Both test groups showed reduced blood glucose levels, with the group taking the apple cider vinegar showing a higher reduction in blood glucose than the group taking the pills. The researchers concluded there is a therapeutic effect for vinegar in adults that are at risk for developing type 2 diabetes (18).

There is the potential for prescription drug interactions when using apple cider vinegar and the chromium in the ACV can affect insulin levels in the blood, so always consult with your doctor prior to adding ACV to your diet if you are diabetic or suspect you may be diabetic. The studies thus far are promising, but they've been on small test groups and there's serious need for further research before any conclusions can be drawn.

Energy

Have you been feeling run down or down in the dumps lately? Do you have trouble recovering quickly from tough physical fitness sessions? Do you find yourself feeling tired partway through the day and need an energy boost to make it through to the evening?

If you answered yes to any of these questions, apple cider vinegar may be able to help. Instead of turning to expensive energy drinks that do more harm than they do good, try an all-natural solution.

Apple cider vinegar can help you make it through the day because it's packed full of amino acids and electrolytes that give you energy and help counteract the lactic acid that builds up in the body when you've physically exerted yourself (19). The effects are longer-lasting than with energy drinks and there's no let-down like there is when you come down from all of the sugar and caffeine in energy drinks and coffee.

For an added energy boost, try the following concoction:

- **1 cup water.**
- **2 tablespoons raw honey.**
- **1 tablespoon apple cider vinegar.**
- **1 teaspoon shredded ginger root.**

This tonic may not taste great, but it may be able to provide you the energy you need to make it through a difficult day.

Gout

Gout is a painful, and sometime debilitating, joint condition caused when uric acid crystals form in the joints. Under normal conditions, uric acid is processed by the kidneys and passed out of the body, but some people have high levels of uric acid in their blood. This leads to crystallization of the acid in the joints. Uric acid crystals irritate the joints and cause inflammation, which leads to moderate to severe joint pain. A gout attack usually lasts 5 to 10 days, but can last longer. Sufferers of gout often go through bouts where they live a normal life followed by weeks or months of intense pain when they have a flare-up.

A number of sources claim apple cider vinegar is able to relieve gout because the malic acid in the vinegar dissolves the crystals that have formed in the joints (20). Other sources claim ACV works on gout because it turns the body alkaline and creates an environment in which gout is unable to grow (21). To date, there have been no scientific studies on the connection between apple cider vinegar and gout, but it's a well-known home remedy.

What probably happens is apple cider vinegar acts on the body in a number of beneficial ways that ease gout pain and help prevent it from reoccurring. As it rebalances the system toward better health, one of the changes made may be an enhanced ability to process uric acid. Instead of having to store it away in the joints, the body is able to process it and rid itself of the unneeded acid.

It isn't recommended that you use apple cider vinegar as the sole treatment for a case of gout that is currently underway, as serious joint damage can occur in severe cases. ACV may, however, be able to be used in conjunction with conventional treatments to both speed up the elimination of gout and prevent reoccurrences.

A tablespoon or two of apple cider vinegar in a cup of water once a day seems to be a common dosage used by those looking to eliminate gout. In addition to the vinegar, try drinking more water and less alcohol. Drinking more water and giving up alcoholic beverages will allow your body to more effectively flush uric acid out of your system (22).

Gut Health

The human body operates as an integrated ecosystem. Imbalances in the gut can cause problems in other areas of the body, with symptoms that manifest themselves in areas of the body that aren't normally associated with an unhealthy gut. Western doctors tend to diagnose symptoms instead of looking at the big picture, so gut problems often go undiagnosed until they get really bad or gastrointestinal symptoms start to arise.

Digestive issues like irritable bowels, diarrhea, stomachaches and bloating are the easiest to diagnose because they're tied directly to the gut. What many people don't realize is other symptoms they may be having like allergies, pain in their joints, liver problems and autoimmune diseases could also be cropping up as a result of an unhealthy gut.

So what exactly is an unhealthy gut?

The Western diet is largely devoid of probiotic bacteria, which are critical to good gut health. Probiotic bacteria are beneficial bacteria that aid with digestion and promote nutrient absorption. When these bacteria are present in large amounts, the gut is in good health. Eating probiotic foods can help restore beneficial flora to the gut.

Bad bacteria and yeasts can thrive when beneficial flora are lacking. The absence of good bacteria can allow harmful bacteria and yeasts like candida to gain a foothold and start growing out of control. Instead of helping your body, bad bacteria wreak havoc on your body. Digestive issues can occur and your body may initiate an immune system response to combat the effects of the bacteria. This leaves fewer immune system resources available to combat other issues, and is the reason why symptoms of poor gut health can pop up anywhere in your body.

This imbalance of bad to good bacteria can be compounded by use of antibiotics. These drugs kill all bacteria in the body, leaving the gut wide open for bad bugs to take control. Consuming large amounts of simple carbs and sugars feeds the bad bacteria, making it more likely bad bacteria are going to grow back as opposed to good bacteria.

Do enough research into natural remedies for gut health and digestive issues and you'll see apple cider vinegar recommended again and again. There aren't any studies to back this claim up, but there's quite a bit of anecdotal evidence and the science behind these claims is sound.

Apple cider vinegar contains **pectin**, which is a prebiotic carbohydrate that binds to unhealthy items in the digestive tract. Cholesterol, harmful bacteria and toxins are just some of the items pectin can bind to. Once pectin sticks to something, it's whisked away and eliminated via bowel movement (23).

This can help clear out bad bacteria in the gut, leaving room for beneficial bacteria, which are also found in apple cider vinegar (24). To further boost the level of good bacteria in the gut, try to consume probiotic foods rich in healthy bacteria and you'll be well on your way to restoring your gut to good health.

Candida and Yeast Infections

Candida is a fungus and a form of yeast that exists in small amounts in everyone's digestive system and mouth. It helps the body break down and digest food. The key is to keep candida under control. An unhealthy gut can lead to an explosion in the growth of candida, or what's known as a **yeast infection**.

Under normal conditions, the good bacteria in the gut keep candida in check. However, there are times when the good bacteria in the gut can die off, opening the door for candida to grow unchecked. Once it starts to grow to large numbers, candida is extremely difficult to get back under control. The best defense against candida is to never let it get out of control in the first place.

The following factors are some of the leading factors known to promote candida overgrowth:

- **Antibiotics.** When antibiotics are used, both good and bad bacteria are killed off. This can allow candida to take over once the antibiotics are stopped.
- **Eating refined carbs.** A diet high in sugars, alcohol and/or other refined carbs provides candida with food they can use as fuel to expand their population.
- **Lack of probiotic foods in the diet.** Failure to eat probiotic foods leaves a void in the gut because you aren't consuming the good bacteria your body needs. Candida can step in and fill this void in no time at all.

- **Oral contraceptives.** The use of birth control pills can influence candida growth.

Yeast infections are often **systemic infections**, meaning they can spread throughout the entire body. The growth starts in the gut and breaks out of the intestines and enters the bloodstream. Once it makes its way into the bloodstream, symptoms can manifest themselves anywhere in the body.

If you're suffering from any of the following symptoms, you may have candida overgrowth:

- **Anxiety.**
- **Athlete's foot.**
- **Autoimmune diseases.**
- **Depression.**
- **Digestive problems.**
- **Dizziness.**
- **Fatigue.**
- **Itching in the genitals.**
- **Lack of ability to focus.**
- **Mood swings.**
- **Nail fungus or infections.**
- **Nausea.**
- **Severe allergies.**
- **Skin infections.**
- **Sugar cravings.**
- **Vaginal and urinary tract infections.**

These are just a sampling of the many symptoms that can crop up as a result of a candida overgrowth. Since Western doctors tend to diagnose the symptoms instead of the health of the overall system, candida overgrowth can go undiagnosed for years while the symptoms get worse and worse.

A common misconception is that only women can suffer from yeast infections. For obvious reasons, only women can suffer from a *vaginal* yeast infection, but men can suffer from candida overgrowth and can experience a number of the symptoms. They can harbor the yeast in their genitals and pass it on to women they have sexual contact with without them ever knowing it.

Treating a candida overgrowth is complex and isn't as simple as adding apple cider vinegar to one's diet. It often takes weeks or even months of eating right to reverse the overgrowth and bring things back under control. Apple cider vinegar can be part of a natural therapy regime, but it isn't likely to work if other changes aren't made. The key is to make changes that restore healthy bacteria to the gut while ridding it of candida.

The first change most people need to make is to switch their diets. Eliminate alcohol, sugars and refined flours because they feed candida. Getting rid of candida's main food sources will go a long way toward controlling growth. While you're at it, stop eating unhealthy trans fats and refined vegetable oils.

Now, add foods containing probiotic bacteria to your diet. These foods contain beneficial bacteria that you want in your gut. Fermented foods like yogurt, kefir and fermented fruits and vegetables are all good choices. Make sure the fermented foods have live and active cultures or you're wasting your time.

Unrefined coconut oil and apple cider vinegar can be added to your diet to help kill off the candida (25). The coconut oil contains substances that perforate the cell walls of the candida, while the apple cider vinegar creates an environment that isn't conducive to candida growth.

When the candida starts to die off, the body can react in an unpredictable manner. You may experience fatigue, headaches and a number of other symptoms associated with the die-off.

Serious system-wide candida overgrowth may not be able to be eliminated through use of natural solutions. If you suspect you have a systemic yeast infection, seek medical advice prior to attempting to rid yourself of it using apple cider vinegar.

Heartburn

Here's a use of apple cider vinegar that doesn't make sense at first glance. Apple cider vinegar is an effective home remedy for heartburn. Since it's packed full of acids, you'd think it would be the last thing you'd want to drink when experiencing heartburn, but if the thousands of people who swear by it are to be believed, it's an effective home remedy.

This is one treatment I can vouch for myself. When I eat certain foods, I end up with mild to severe acid reflux. It can last for hours on end and antacids and over-the-counter acid reflux medications provide little relief, if any. Even when they work to ease the burning, antacids simply mask the pain, doing nothing to actually solve the underlying problems causing the acid reflux.

I got fed up one day and started researching natural solutions for heartburn. I stumbled across apple cider vinegar and decided to try it because I had a container in the pantry. I have to admit I was skeptical at first and expected the burning sensation I was feeling to get worse after taking the apple cider vinegar, but within minutes the intense burning started to subside. To my surprise, the heartburn stayed gone for hours

The exact reason apple cider vinegar works so well for heartburn isn't known, as there haven't been any studies to date that look at the connection between apple cider vinegar and acid reflux. That hasn't stopped people from coming up with their own reasons as to why it works.

One of the more interesting theories is that vinegar tightens the muscle at the bottom of the esophagus, effectively preventing the acids from forcing their way up. This makes sense because heartburn is caused by acids making their way into the esophagus and burning everything they come in contact with. If they can't get in, there will be no irritation and no burn.

Another theory involves the mother of bacteria and the live cultures that exist in the vinegar. These probiotic cultures may compete with bad bacteria in the gut, displacing them and helping prevent GERD caused by the bad bacteria. Additionally, the enzymes that exist along with the mother aid with digestion. The stomach creates excess acid when it comes time to digest large meals, which can lead to heartburn. Consume ACV before a meal and the enzymes may take over, eliminating the need for more acid. Some people claim taking probiotic supplements along with the apple cider vinegar is more effective than vinegar alone.

The effect of vinegar on heartburn may also be due to the alkalizing effect vinegar has once it's inside the body. As the vinegar is processed, it may balance out some of the acids in the stomach and make heartburn less likely to occur. The acetic acid in vinegar isn't as strong as hydrochloric acid found in your stomach, so yet another theory is it may dilute the acid in your stomach, rendering it less potent.

Acid reflux is sometimes caused when the stomach doesn't produce *enough* acid to digest the food that's being consumed. The food sits in the stomach undigested and the stomach fills up. Once the stomach gets too full, what little acid there is in the stomach can be pushed to the top of the stomach where it leaks into the esophagus, causing acid reflux. Consuming ACV adds acid to the stomach and aids with digestion, which may get rid of the food before it can stack up and start to push out acid.

Be aware that there are stomach conditions that can cause acid reflux for which apple cider vinegar isn't a good solution. Apple cider vinegar doesn't work well for acid reflux caused by hearth problems. Ulcers can cause acid regurgitation and consuming ACV to try and treat acid reflux caused by ulcers could actually irritate the ulcers and make the symptoms worse. If bloating occurs after consuming apple cider vinegar, discontinue use of apple cider vinegar immediately.

Always consult with your physician prior to using apple cider vinegar as a home remedy for heartburn. It's important to make sure you don't have underlying conditions that could be made worse by the acids in the vinegar.

While these are all good theories, they're just that. Theories. The true causes of acid reflux and the reasons apple cider vinegar works to treat most likely comes down to a combination of factors. Here's to hoping there are studies in the works that seek to prove apple cider vinegar an effective solution for heartburn.

Mineral Absorption

Sometimes eating foods high in vitamins and minerals isn't enough. The foods you eat can, at times, pass through your digestive system before the body has a chance to process the minerals. This usually happens because the body has trouble digesting the food and extracting the minerals from it.

A Japanese study published in 2006 showed the addition of acetic acid to the diet of rats led to an increase in the uptake of minerals. Calcium, magnesium and phosphorus intake all improved significantly when the rats were fed a diet containing acetic acid (26). A similar study done in 1999 had similar results. When rats in this study were fed a diet containing 1.6% vinegar, calcium uptake increased (27).

Consuming apple cider vinegar prior to a meal is thought to have the same effect in humans. Since ACV is full of acetic acid, it likely improves your ability to absorb minerals from the foods you eat and transport them to the areas of your body where they're needed. Consuming as much as a tablespoon of ACV mixed with water prior to mealtime may improve your body's ability to digest foods and pull minerals out of them.

This is especially critical when it comes to foods that are full of calcium because they often contain compounds that aren't conducive to mineral absorption. Leafy green veggies are high in calcium, but contain compounds that partially block calcium absorption. Eating a salad with a teaspoon or two of apple cider vinegar sprinkled over it may be the added boost the body needs to maximize calcium absorption.

Milk and milk products are also high in calcium, but the lactose in the milk makes it difficult to digest. Vinegar may be able to help the body digest milk and take in the calcium from the milk products being consumed. It's best to consume fermented milk products like kefir and yogurt because they also contain digestive enzymes that help the body process the lactose.

Hiccups

Hic . . . Hic . . . Hic . . . . . Hiccup.

A mild case of hiccups can usually be waited out, but did you know the longest recorded case of hiccups was 68 years? A man named Charles Osborne was unfortunate enough to contract a case of hiccups that lasted from 1922 until 1990, placing him in firm control of a record I'm sure nobody else in the world wants to break. It's believed this case of hiccups was due to a blood vessel bursting in the area of Osborne's brain responsible for controlling hiccups.

While apple cider vinegar probably wouldn't have helped alleviate Mr. Osborne's case of hiccups, it can sometimes help with milder cases. The acids in ACV are believed to soothe the nerves in your mouth and throat that are responsible for hiccups, stopping them dead in their tracks.

Try sipping a cup of warm water with a teaspoon of apple cider vinegar mixed in to see if it helps. Some sources recommend taking a teaspoon of vinegar straight, but I think I'd rather deal with the hiccups. Then again, if I had a case that lasted more than about 5 minutes, I'd be willing to try almost anything to get rid of them.

Cases of hiccups that last more than 48 hours may be a symptom of a serious medical condition. These hiccups, known as **persistent hiccups**, can last days, weeks, months or, in Osborne's case, almost a lifetime. They can be brought about by diseases that affect the nervous system, cancer, metabolic health issues and diseases that affect the brain.

Seek immediate medical attention if you have a case of hiccups that won't go away.

Leg Cramps

It usually starts with a tell-tale twinge. When that twinge turns into a full-on leg cramp, it can be agonizing. While most cramps are short-lived, some people are more prone to them than others and can suffer multiple periods in which their legs cramp up at night when they're trying to sleep. Cramps are the result of powerful muscle contractions in the legs. Doctors aren't sure exactly why they occur, but they've been tied to physical exertion, poor diet and dehydration, amongst other things.

Apple cider vinegar is one of the oldest known remedies for leg cramps. Add a tablespoon of apple cider vinegar and a tablespoon of raw honey to a cup of water and drink it and relief may soon be on its way. ACV is thought to work well for cramps because of the minerals and other nutrients it contains.

This method probably works best when done on a continuous basis, as the nutrients will already be in the body from the previous night. If cramps persist, seek medical attention, as the cramps could be caused by an underlying medical condition.

Weight Loss

Dr. D.C. Jarvis first mentioned apple cider vinegar as a dietary aid in his 1950's folk medicine book. He theorized taking apple cider vinegar would boost metabolism by causing fat to be burned instead of stored. As it turns out, he wasn't too far off in his postulation, as there are a growing number of studies that appear to show apple cider vinegar to be an effective dietary aid.

A Japanese study on mice, published in 2009 by the Central Research Institute in Japan, found that mice that were administered acetic acid showed suppressed accumulation of body fat and liver lipids (28).

This initial study led to a 2009 study of obese Japanese people, which concluded consumption of vinegar is associated with lower body weight and a decrease in appetite (29). The latter study is titled "Vinegar Intake Reduces Body Weight, Body Fat Mass, and Serum Triglyceride Levels in Obese Japanese Subjects" and is available for free at the following the web address:

https://www.jstage.jst.go.jp/article/bbb/73/8/73_90231/_pdf

Study participants were divided into three groups and were administered 15 ml, 30 ml or a placebo containing 0 ml of apple cider vinegar daily. Both of the groups receiving the vinegar showed a significant decrease in body mass index (BMI), body weight, visceral and subcutaneous fat area, waist circumference and serum triglyceride levels in comparison to the placebo group. The 30 ml group outperformed the 15 ml group (Ibid.).

The results were gradual and didn't start to accelerate until after the 4th week of consumption of apple cider vinegar, so don't expect instant results. The highest dosage in the Japanese experiment was 30 ml, which is equal to approximately 6 teaspoons (or two tablespoons) of vinegar (Ibid.). This dosage could be achieved by adding a couple teaspoons of vinegar to a cup of water and drinking it three times a day. One of the cups of water and vinegar could be eliminated by drizzling 2 teaspoons of ACV over a salad and eating the salad.

Vinegar has been shown to increase satiety when consumed with meals. A study published in the European Journal of Clinical Nutrition in 2005 served white bread with 50g of carbohydrates to participants and had them consume varying amounts of vinegar with the bread. The test showed lowered blood glucose response in the participants who consumed vinegar and the participants who consumed the vinegar said they felt fuller than those who didn't (30).

Another study used apple cider vinegar combined with a number of other dietary supplements like alfalfa and wheat grass to create a green drink that was consumed once a day, along with a cleansing supplement and probiotic and prebiotic supplements. The study found patients that stuck to the diet and regimented supplementation program lost weigh and had lower cholesterol and blood pressure (31).

While the results of all of these studies are promising, it's highly unlikely simply adding apple cider vinegar to a person's diet is going to result in rapid or pronounced weight loss. It isn't a magic weight loss formula, but does appear to have its applications when it comes to dieting. Adding vinegar to a poor diet probably won't get people the results they want. Adding it to a healthy diet and combining that with regular exercise may be the key.

Based on the findings of the studies, it appears consuming apple cider vinegar just prior to or even during meal time is the most effective approach. The evidence suggests you'll suppress your appetite, help the body monitor glucose and the enzymes in the vinegar will aid with digestion. That's a combination of factors that's tough to beat.

Skin

All the uses of apple cider vinegar discussed thus far have been for internal issues, so it might surprise you to find ACV also works to keep the outside of your body in good shape. It's used as a remedy for a number of skin conditions and can be used to promote good overall skin and pore health.

Scarlett Johansson reportedly uses apple cider vinegar to keep her skin in good shape. In the February 2013 edition of Elle Magazine, Scarlett admitted to using apple cider vinegar to heal her skin. She has an amazing complexion, so the apple cider vinegar must be doing her at least some good. It wouldn't be a big surprise to hear other celebrities have it hidden in their bag of tricks as well.

Acne

Acne is, by far, the most prevalent skin disease in the world. Rare is the person who has never suffered an acne flare-up. It can appear anywhere on the body, but is usually most prevalent on the face, chest and the back. For the lucky folks amongst us, acne comes on at puberty and passes as they enter adulthood, but all of us aren't so lucky. For some, acne is a lifelong affliction that requires constant treatment to keep it in check.

Acne forms when a pore in the skin becomes blocked and the sebum the pore produces gets trapped beneath the skin. Bacteria begins to grow in the blocked pore and one of two things happens: the sebum and bacteria stay below the surface of the pore and a **whitehead** forms or the sebum and bacteria rise to the surface of the pore and form into a **blackhead**. If the follicle wall ruptures at any time, the bacteria and sebum are released into the skin and an infection occurs. This causes inflammation and a pimple forms.

The natural antibacterial properties of apple cider vinegar may be able to help you eliminate acne at the source. Applying it topically will help kill the bacteria known to cause acne. It can also help with the inflammation associated with acne, but be aware applying it to open pimples does sting. Combine one part ACV with 2 parts water and apply it to the affected area.

Apple cider vinegar can also be used as spot treatment for existing pimples. As soon as you feel one starting to form, apply apple cider vinegar to it a couple times a day.

The swelling should go down and the pimple should quickly become an afterthought.

Don't expect immediate results. It can take weeks for apple cider vinegar to help with acne—and things might get worse in the short-term. Apple cider vinegar gets deeps inside the pores and is thought to pull impurities to the surface, so more acne may be the short-term result as the impurities are purged. People who have waited out this short-term increase in acne claim to have had clearer skin as a result. There are a handful of people who state their skin never cleared up or got worse when they started using ACV, but it isn't clear how long they waited for the acne to clear.

Consuming apple cider internally at the same time you're applying it to your skin for acne may help balance your body's internal systems and help eliminate acne from that angle as well.

Age Spots

Age spots, also known as liver spots because at one time they were thought to be associated with liver problems, are blemishes on the skin that often appear due to prolonged exposure to the UV rays of the sun over the course of one's life. They can range in color from light brown to black and typically appear in areas of the body that have seen the most sun, but can appear anywhere.

Most liver spots aren't dangerous and pose no threat to the person who has them. They are, however, unsightly and people aren't happy when they develop. In extreme cases, people may turn to cosmetic surgery to get rid of them, but that probably isn't necessary when you consider the natural home remedies available.

Aloe Vera gel is said to reduce the visual appearance of age spots. Applying the gel 2 to 3 times a day may help heal the skin and diminish the spots.

Apple cider vinegar is also said to eliminate age spots. Some people use it on its own, while others mix it with onion juice prior to application. To use it on its own, apply apple cider vinegar to the age spot using a Q-Tip or cotton ball. Hold or affix the cotton ball in place and leave it there for 30 minutes.

Follow these directions to use apple cider vinegar and onion juice together:

1. **Place an onion in the blender and blend it up.**
2. **Pour the contents of the blender into a piece of cheesecloth and squeeze the onion juice out of it.**

3. **Combine equal parts apple cider vinegar and onion juice.**
4. **Soak a cotton ball in the solution.**
5. **Hold or affix the cotton ball in place for 20 to 30 minutes.**
6. **Apply daily until the liver spot fades away.**

Be aware this is a strong solution and has the potential to burn the skin in sensitive individuals. Use it at your own risk. Keep it away from your eyes.

Corns and Calluses

Corns and calluses are painful thickenings of the skin in areas where excessive rubbing occurs, usually on the hands or the feet. People who wear work boots or tight-fitting shoes get them frequently and they can become painful in a hurry. **Corns** are raised areas of thick skin that are conical in shape, while **calluses** are flatter discs of thick skin.

A number of medical products are available to chemically remove corns and calluses. These products usually use **salicylic acid** to eat the corn or callus away. Other people attempt to cut or file them away. Cutting or filing isn't safe to do at home and should only be done by a medical professional.

To get rid of corns and calluses naturally, soak your feet for 30 minutes in a gallon of warm water with a cup of ACV added to it. Dry the affected area and use a pumice stone to remove any loose material. Soak a bandage in apple cider vinegar and affix it to the corn or callus and leave it on overnight. Repeat this routine until the corn or callus is gone.

This technique works best on smaller corns and calluses and may not completely get rid of larger ones. If corns or calluses are appearing due to rubbing, it's important to get rid of the root cause or they may return with a vengeance.

Deodorant

This may seem like a strange use for apple cider vinegar since it smells like my gym bag at the end of the week, but ACV can actually be used as deodorant. It naturally eliminates bad smells, including those found in stinky armpits and other areas of the body that stink.

Simply apply a small amount of apple cider to your armpits and rub it in. It'll smell like vinegar for a few minutes and all bad smells will be eliminated once the scent of the vinegar dissipates. If you're concerned about the smell of the vinegar, try adding a few drops of your favorite essential oil or oil blend to the ACV.

You'll smell great all day and won't have to worry about the aluminum and other compounds found in commercial deodorants.

Face Wash and Toner

Apple cider vinegar contains acids and other compounds that make it both antibacterial and antifungal by nature. They cleanse and tone the skin, while helping to naturally remove dead skin cells. ACV helps regulate the pH of the skin and keeps sebum production balanced, so the skin doesn't become too dry or too oily.

To use apple cider vinegar as face wash, mix 1 part ACV to 2 parts water in a small bowl. Splash warm water on your face to open up your pores and follow it up by wiping your face clean with a cotton ball dipped in the ACV solution. Let it sit on your face for a minute or two before wiping it off using a clean cotton ball. Alternatively, you can apply it and leave it on your skin. Be careful not to let it run into your eyes or you're going to be sorry.

Those with sensitive skin can reduce the amount of ACV they mix with the water, while others may want to up the amount of vinegar used. Some people use apple cider vinegar as face wash and toner both when they wake up in the morning and when they go to bed in the evening. Others have found it works best for them when they only use it once a day.

Everyone's skin is different, so it may take some playing around to get things right.

Poison Oak and Ivy

If you spend any amount of time hiking around in the country, you've probably had a run-in (or two or ten) with poison oak or ivy. I grew up in a country town and it seems like somebody was always getting into a patch of the "itchy stuff," as we used to call it.

We didn't know it then, but the itching and burning you experience when your skin comes in contact with poison oak or ivy is due to an oily sap called **urushiol** that exists on all exposed surfaces of the plant. It's this sap that causes the allergic reaction and you don't even have to come in direct contact with the plant to get infected. Anything the plant has touched or brushed against will have urushiol on it and can cause a reaction if it comes in contact with bare skin.

The urushiol remains on the plant after it dies and can even irritate the lungs if the plant is burned. In fact, inhaling smoke containing urushiol is even more dangerous than touching it, as it can do a number on your respiratory system.

ACV can be used to relieve the itching and burning associated with poison oak and ivy. Combine equal parts ACV and water in a spray bottle and spray it onto the affected area. The itching should stop immediately. Apply aloe gel to further promote healing.

Sunburn

Everybody knows the cost of spending too much time in the sun. You tell yourself you're going to remember to reapply sunscreen midday, but then you get to having fun and before you know it you're bright red. It would be easy to stop a sunburn in its tracks if you felt the burn as it was happening, but that isn't the case. Instead, it can take hours after getting too much sun for the pain to kick in.

By that time, it's too late and you're already in for a miserable time.

The next time you get sunburnt and want to shorten the duration of the burn, there are a couple of natural solutions that work hand-in-hand to get rid of the pain and to shorten duration of the sunburn.

When you first realize you have a sunburn, it's time for an apple cider vinegar bath. Add 2 to 3 cups of ACV to the bathwater as you fill it up. Be careful not to make the water too warm or climbing in is going to be excruciating. Soak in the tub for up to 20 minutes and when you get out, most of the pain should have vanished. Alternatively, you can soak strips of gauze or cotton cloth in a solution made by mixing ½ cup of ACV with 2 cups of cool water and apply them to the burn. Others prefer to put the solution in a spray bottle and mist it onto the sunburnt area.

Follow this up by coating the burn with pure aloe vera gel. Massage it into the area of the sunburn to promote healing and shorten how long the sunburn lasts. Coconut oil also works well, but it's a bit on the greasy side.

This method works best on mild to moderate sunburns. If the sunburn is bad enough to blister, seek medical attention. Do not apply apple cider vinegar or aloe gel to a sunburn that has blistered, as it'll do more harm than good. If you feel dizzy or have a fever, it's especially critical to get to a doctor since that could be a sign of more serious health conditions like heat exhaustion or heat stroke.

Varicose Veins

Varicose veins are distended veins that have grown in size and bulge out from the skin. They don't just look bad, they can cause aches and pains, muscle cramps and feelings of heaviness in the legs. They're more prevalent in older people and people packing extra pounds, but people of any age can get them.

The following factors can contribute to growth of varicose veins:

- **Age.**
- **Heavy lifting.**
- **Hormonal changes.**
- **Lack of exercise.**
- **Poor diet.**
- **Pregnancy.**
- **Prolonged time spent standing or sitting.**
- **Tight clothing.**
- **Weight.**

Medical treatments are available that will help minimize varicose veins. Compounds can be injected into the vessel to cause it to shrink. Laser surgery is an option for some, but it tends to be expensive. Larger varicose veins may require surgical excision. Treatments tend to be expensive and may require multiple visits to the doctor.

Apple cider vinegar is a home remedy that's thought to work to reduce varicose veins. Mix a cup of apple cider vinegar into a cup of water and apply it to affected area of the legs using a soft cloth. Repeat the application a couple times a day. The ACV can help relieve the swelling associated with varicose veins and may improve circulation in the cell wall, causing the varicose vein to disappear over time.

Warts

NOTE: The information in this section doesn't apply to genital warts. Never attempt to get rid of genital warts by applying apple cider vinegar to them.

A wart is a skin growth caused by a virus that exists in most people. The **human papillomavirus (HPV)** can cause the top layer of skin to start rapidly growing, creating a wart in the process. Warts can grow anywhere on the body, but are most-commonly found on the hands and feet. Some warts will go away after a few months, while others can last for years.

Many people claim to have used apple cider vinegar to get rid of warts. A common technique is to soak a piece of cotton big enough to cover the wart in apple cider vinegar and then affix it to the wart with a bandage or medical tape. Leave it on for at least 12 hours. When you reach the 12-hour mark, you can either swap out the cotton ball for a fresh one or let the wart air out for 12 hours before putting a new cotton ball on.

Repeat this process until the wart dries up and falls off. It can take weeks before the wart disappears.

Hair & Scalp

Are you suffering from itchy scalp, dandruff or dull, lifeless hair that breaks easily and may be thinning? If so, you might want to give apple cider vinegar a try to see if it can help. The evidence in favor of ACV as a treatment for hair and scalp conditions is mostly anecdotal, but there are a lot of people who swear by it.

In order to get an understanding of why ACV works so well on hair, let's take a quick look at the anatomy of a strand of hair. Hair grows from a **hair follicle**. It forms at the base of the follicle and is pushed out of the skin via an opening at the top of the follicle. Each hair follicle has a **sebaceous gland** attached to it, which is responsible for lubing the hair as it moves through the follicle. The oil the hair is lubed with is known as **sebum**.

The part of the hair that leaves the body is known as the **hair shaft**. The hair shaft is made up of dead cells known as **keratin** and material that binds the keratin together. Cut a hair shaft in half and look at it under a microscope and you'll find it has either two or three layers. Some pieces of hair have an inside layer known as the **medulla**, while others are missing this layer. The next layer is the **cortex layer**. This is the layer responsible for determining the color, texture and durability of your hair.

The outer layer, known as the **cuticle**, is tasked with protecting the inner layers. The cuticles are like little shingles and can open and close to let moisture in and to keep environmental hazards out. Over time, the cuticle layer can get damaged and the cuticles can become rough. Cuticles that are slightly lifted allow substances into the hair even when they're closed. They also allow moisture trapped inside the hair to escape, drying out the hair.

When the cuticles are sealed tightly, they lock moisture in the hair and keep environmental contaminants out. Hair with tightly closed cuticles appears vibrant and alive. Failing to close the cuticles can leave hair looking dull, lifeless and it will be more prone to breakage.

People with curly hair have cuticles that are slightly open. It's especially important for these people to use products that close the cuticles.

The acids in ACV close up the cuticles, making hair strands less likely to dehydrate and suffer damage from external factors. When the cuticles are closed, the hair becomes more manageable and tends to have a lustrous shine.

Balance Hair's pH

Human hair is slightly acidic by nature. The sebaceous glands in the hair follicle release a slightly acidic oil called sebum that coats each strand of hair as it leaves the follicle. The natural acidity of hair theoretically should keep harmful bacteria at bay and the natural acids existing on the hair and scalp should keep the cuticles of healthy hair sealed tightly shut.

The slightly acidic nature of hair is problematic because a number of hair products sold in stores are more alkaline than the natural pH of hair. These products strip the protective sebum away from the hair, leaving it open to damage. Using alkaline hair products causes the cuticles to open up, and they may stay open and allow moisture to escape. Leaving cuticles open like this can cause long-term damage and color loss to the hair.

The following problems can occur when the pH of your hair is out of balance:

- **Bacterial infections.**
- **Dandruff.**
- **Dry or damaged hair.**
- **Frizzy hair.**
- **Fungal infections.**
- **Loss of color.**
- **Tangles.**

There are expensive hair care products on the market that can be used to balance the pH of your hair. They probably work, but apple cider vinegar is able to do the same thing naturally and for a lot less money. Once you're done washing and conditioning your hair, apply a tablespoon or two of apple cider vinegar mixed into a cup of water to your hair and let it sit for a few minutes. Rinse it out with cold water and you'll have just treated your hair with a slightly acidic treatment that can help rebalance the pH.

NOTE: There may be some confusion after reading this section because people consume apple cider vinegar as a supplement to rebalance their internal system toward alkalinity. Apple cider vinegar is a strange substance, in that it's acidic by nature, but once consumed creates an alkaline environment. To be clear, applying it to the skin and hair creates a slightly acidic environment.

Clarify

Commercial hair products, chlorine and hard water can all leave residue behind that builds up over time. Dirt and grime sticks to this residue, further compounding the problem. This residue can leave hair feeling weighed down, greasy and difficult to manage.

Clarifying shampoo can be used to remove the residue, but it tends to be expensive and is full of harsh chemicals.

Apple cider vinegar may be a better option because it gently strips the residue from hair. It's works great for removing hard water residue from hair because it dissolves the minerals on contact. It isn't as good at removing oily build-up, but can still strip at least some of it away.

If you have a lot of residue already built up in your hair, you might want to use clarifying shampoo one time to get it out and then maintain your hair with apple cider vinegar. You might not be able to completely eliminate clarifying shampoo from your conditioning regime, but using ACV should allow you to space your clarifying shampoo sessions out so they're few and far between.

To clarify hair with ACV, add a quarter cup of vinegar to two cups of water. Massage it into the hair and cover the hair with a shower cap. Let it sit for 15 minutes before rinsing the ACV out with cold water.

Dandruff & Itchy Scalp

Bottle bacillus is the type of bacteria that's usually responsible for dandruff and itchy scalp. When the pH of the scalp is imbalanced, bottle bacillus and other harmful bacteria and yeasts can start to grow unchecked, wreaking havoc on the skin and the hair follicles. Hair follicles get clogged, sebum and dead skin cells accumulate and large flakes form that fall off when the scalp is disturbed.

Half a cup of apple cider vinegar mixed into a cup of water can be used as a scalp treatment for dandruff. Pull the hair aside and massage the vinegar solution directly into the scalp. Leave it in for 15 minutes and rinse it out with cool water. Repeat daily for 5 to 7 days, or until the dandruff is gone. Keep an eye out for signs of dandruff coming back and reapply the solution at the first sign of flakes.

Alternatively, you can treat your scalp with ACV once a week to keep dandruff from coming back. Increase the number of treatments if you start to see flakes. Everyone's hair is different, so it may take some experimentation to find the right number of weekly or monthly treatments to eliminate dandruff.

The ACV is believed to rebalance the pH of the scalp, creating an environment that isn't conducive for harmful bacteria and yeast to grow. It kills off the bacteria and stimulates the hair follicles to produce sebum in normal amounts.

A few drops of tea tree oil can be added for additional relief. Tea tree essential oil is both antifungal and antibacterial and can help eliminate the microbes causing the dandruff.

If dandruff persists or gets worse, seek medical attention. There may be an underlying medical condition causing the dandruff that needs to be addressed.

Detangler

Damaged hair can be difficult to detangle. The raised cuticles on the hair shafts catch on one another and the friction causes a tangled, knotted mess. This is especially common in naturally curly hair because the cuticles are already slightly raised.

Try adding apple cider vinegar to your hair to make detangling easier. First, mist your hair with cold water (or rinse it with cold water if you're just getting out of the shower). Mix a cup of ACV into two cups of cool water and place it in spray bottle. Pick a section of hair and spray it with ACV. Start from the end and slowly comb out the knots.

For badly knotted hair that ACV alone can't untangle, try adding a bit of coconut oil to your fingers and massaging it into each strand of hair as you detangle it. The ACV will seal the cuticles, making your hair less likely to get caught as it slides across itself, and the coconut oil will lube the hair and make all but the worst of knots slide right out.

Hair Growth

Here's a use for apple cider vinegar that may surprise you. It's used to promote hair growth in people who have thinning hair. There are a number of people who swear it works and have seen lost hair start to grow back after using ACV on their head.

Does it work?

Well, like most apple cider vinegar remedies, scientists haven't studies this one, but there's a lot of anecdotal evidence that says it does. There aren't many people claiming ACV regrew them a full head of hair, but there are quite a few who claim it's helped them grow back at least some hair.

Based on what we already know about ACV, we can conclude it might work, depending largely on the reason the hair is falling out in the first place. We know ACV balances the pH of the scalp and helps clear out clogged follicles. This alone could be enough to stimulate some hair growth, as the clogged follicles may start producing hair again once they've been cleared out.

Exfoliating the scalp can help even more, as it clears out more of the built-up skin and residue that can clog follicles. Combine 2 tablespoons of brown sugar with 2 tablespoons of coconut oil and massage it into your scalp with a toothbrush to exfoliate and get rid of dead skin cells. Make sure you cover all areas of your scalp.

Wash your hair as you normally would and follow that up by rinsing it with equal parts apple cider vinegar mixed with water. Repeat this treatment a couple times a week.

Remember that hair grows slowly, so it may take some time before you see results.

Adding a tablespoon of ACV to a cup of water and drinking it once a day may help balance your body internally as well. Hair loss can be due to hormonal imbalances and internal problems, so consuming ACV may be able to help.

Head Lice

Commercial treatments for head lice work to kill the lice, but are full of toxic chemicals you probably don't want on your head . . . Or your children's head, since we all know they're usually the ones who bring lice into the home.

Luckily, there are natural treatments for head lice that are every bit as effective as the toxic commercial shampoos. Apple cider vinegar and coconut oil provide an effective one-two punch that can knock lice out permanently. First, you're going to need a tub of coconut oil and a shower cap. Coat the hair with coconut oil, place the shower cap on and leave the coconut oil in for at least 4 hours. This will kill any lice living in the hair by coating them and suffocating them.

Follow this up by rinsing the hair with a rinse made of half a cup of ACV mixed into 2 cups of water. The rinse will help loosen up the knits, which are eggs that are getting ready to hatch.

The next step's the one everyone hates—combing out the knits. Get one of those knit combs with the tiny teeth and get to it. Make sure you comb every single section of the hair and really pay attention to the base of the hair because that's where lice like to lay their eggs. Pick a section, start at the base and comb the knits out toward the end of the hair. Nits can become detached and float freely around the hair, so it's important you comb the entire head of hair.

It's important to make sure you get all of the nits because the coconut oil treatment doesn't kill the eggs. If you leave eggs behind, they can hatch into new lice that will lay new eggs and start the cycle all over again. This treatment is most effective when it's repeated every few days until no new knits or lice are found.

Household Uses

Apple cider vinegar isn't just great for your body, skin and hair; it can be used around the house as well. It's one of the most versatile natural cleaning compounds in existence and can be used as a disinfectant, a cleanser and a deodorizer. If I could only choose one cleaner to use around the house, apple cider vinegar would be it.

Because ACV is non-toxic and completely natural, it's a good replacement for the harsh chemicals and synthetic additives found in commercial cleaners. Making the switch to apple cider vinegar as a household cleaning product is the smart choice, both in terms of potential health benefits and cost reduction. You'll save money using apple cider vinegar around the house and the people living there will be safer and healthier as a result.

Don't assume just because something isn't listed in this chapter that ACV won't work to clean it. I'm constantly finding new uses for apple cider vinegar around the house. In fact, when a new cleaning task presents itself, ACV is usually the first thing I turn to. I rarely have to look any further.

Always test apple cider vinegar on a small area prior to applying it to the entire surface. There are surfaces that can react negatively to apple cider vinegar and you don't want to find this out after applying it to the entire surface.

All-Purpose ACV Cleaner

Apple cider vinegar has antimicrobial, antifungal and deodorant properties, all of which combine to make it a great all-purpose cleaner that can be used for multiple purposes around the house. You'll be amazed at how many surfaces apple cider vinegar can be used on.

Combine a cup of apple cider vinegar with 2 cups of water in a spray bottle. Spray it on the surface you're looking to clean and wipe it up with a paper towel or soft cloth. For the tougher cleaning jobs, try adding a tablespoon or two of liquid castile soap to the bottle. This solution will make short work of most cleaning tasks.

Bathroom Cleaner

There are a number of areas in the bathroom where apple cider vinegar can be used as an effective cleaning and deodorizing tool. Here are some of the many tasks they can be used for:

Shower Head Declogger

Over time, hard water deposits can build up in the nozzles in the shower head. When the deposits get too large, water flow is impeded and you're left with a shower head that doesn't work the way it was designed to. Next time you're in the shower, look at the shower head. If there are nozzles that are slowly dripping water or aren't dripping water at all, it's time to clear the holes.

Remove the shower head from the shower and place it in a plastic tub filled with half apple cider vinegar and half water. Let the shower head soak for a few hours before returning it to its rightful place atop the shower. This should work to clear out the nozzles, as the ACV dissolves the hard water deposits.

An alternative method of cleaning the shower head involves filling a plastic bag with ACV and water and then affixing the bag over the shower head and leaving it on overnight. This method works well, but doesn't attack the nozzles from both sides like the previous method does.

This same trick can be used to unclog the holes in your iron when it stops putting out steam. Place the iron face-down in enough ACV to cover the bottom of the iron. Let it sit until the holes are unclogged. Alternatively, you can run ACV through the iron.

Shower Doors and Shower Curtains

Apple cider vinegar can be used to clean pretty much the entire shower. Clean glass shower doors with it to leave them free of soap scum, hard water stains and mineral deposits. Wipe the doors clean with newspaper to leave them free of streaks. Shower curtains can also be wiped clean with an ACV solution. For really dirty shower curtains, take them down and toss them in the washing machine with a cup of ACV.

The following areas of the shower/tub can be cleaned with ACV:

- **Doors.**
- **Drains.**
- **Fixtures.**
- **Floor.**
- **Shower curtains.**
- **Tub basin.**
- **Walls.**

All-purpose ACV cleaner can be used for most shower cleaning purposes. Up the strength for the tougher cleaning jobs.

Sink and Counter Cleaner

All-purpose ACV cleaner works great to clean sinks and most countertops. It can also be used to remove hard water stains and mineral deposits from fixtures in the sink.

Toilets

Dump 2 cups of apple cider vinegar into the toilet and let it sit for 30 minutes. Scrub the toilet out with a toilet brush. Use ACV all-purpose cleaner to wipe down the outside of the toilet and the seat.

If you've got hard water rings at the water line in the toilet bowl, you might need to let the ACV soak in the toilet for a longer period of time. Add 3 to 4 cups of apple cider vinegar to the toilet and let it sit for up to 4 hours before attempting to scrub the rings away. If this doesn't work, your only alternative may be to use a pumice stone to scrape away the stains.

Bee and Fly Trap

When summer rolls around, bees and flies can be a real nuisance in some areas. In the summertime, there are days when my house is so full of flies it's tough to think due to all the buzzing and flitting about. My dogs go nuts trying to catch them and it's all-out chaos in the house. Sometimes it seems there are more flies inside than there are outside the house. I'm convinced that for every fly I kill, three flies are sent to take its place.

I love summertime, but there are days when the flies flitting about make me want to move to the Arctic Circle. They don't have flies there, do they?

Escaping outside isn't an option because then you have to deal with the bees. We have both honeybees, which aren't too bad as long as you leave them alone, and yellow jackets, which are some of the orneriest creatures alive. We're constantly killing nests of yellow jackets during the summer, but they still manage to find places to build nests that we can't easily get to.

A bee trap can be used to keep populations of both bees and flies in check. I keep a couple traps inside to help keep the flies in check and multiple traps outside to try and hold the bee and yellow jacket population around my house to reasonable levels.

Experimenting with different solutions to put in the bee trap has revealed the best solution to be one made up of apple cider vinegar, honey and dish soap. The ACV and honey attracts the flying insects into the trap and the dish soap coats their wings and prevents them from flying out.

Mix 1 cup of ACV with 2 tablespoons of honey and a teaspoon of dish soap, add it to the bee trap and watch it fill up with flies and bees. It sure beats running around the house with a rolled-up magazine in hand, swatting like crazy.

Exercise caution when using vinegar and honey to trap bees. This should go without saying, but never approach a nest or hive or you will probably get stung. If you're dealing with a hive of honeybees, consider contacting a beekeeper to relocate the bees instead of killing them. Bee populations are dwindling across the globe and beekeepers are often willing to relocate hives for free or for a nominal fee.

Blinds

Blinds are difficult to clean because it's tough to apply enough pressure to get them clean without bending or otherwise damaging the blinds. By the time you get them sufficiently clean, you're left with blinds that are wavy.

Here's a trick you can use to clean blinds in no time at all. Get an old pair of cotton socks or soft cotton gloves and put them on your hands. Dip the gloves or socks in all-purpose ACV cleaner and wipe down the blinds. It's much easier because you'll have more control than if you were holding a rag soaked in ACV.

Carpet Stain Remover

Carpets can be tough to keep clean, especially if you have light-colored carpets that see a decent amount of foot traffic. Kids, pets and grandkids can really do a number on carpets, leaving a medley of stains in their wake.

Scrubbing stains out of carpet is no fun, no matter how you look at it, but stain removal can be made easier by using apple cider vinegar mixed with water. If there's a spill, first blot up as much of the liquid as you can. Combine equal parts ACV and water in a spray bottle and spray it on the stain. Blot up the ACV and repeat until the stain is gone. Do not rub back and forth as that will spread the stain out. Blotting allows you to lift the stain from the carper without making it bigger.

For stubborn stains that just won't come out, combine a cup of apple cider vinegar with 2 tablespoons of sea salt and 2 tablespoons of borax. This carpet stain remover is able to make short work of most stains. So far, the only stains I've come up against that this cleaner wouldn't lift are blood stains, and hydrogen peroxide can be used on those. Always test any new cleaner you're using on carpet in a small area first, as there is always a risk of fading.

Don't forget to check the manufacturer's cleaning instructions. Certain carpets require specific cleaning ingredients, so make sure you know what works best with your carpet. Failure to follow manufacturer's cleaning instructions can void the warranty on new carpets.

Cleaning Produce

Conventionally-grown produce often arrives in stores covered in pesticide residue. Making the switch to organic produce is an option for some, but organic produce is so expensive it's out of the question for many families. This begs the question what can be done to clear the pesticide residue from produce. You've also got to worry about harmful microorganisms growing on the surface of produce. Bacteria and germs can grow on any produce, regardless of whether it's organic or not.

If you aren't properly washing your produce, you may be putting your health at risk. Apple cider vinegar is an effective cleaner that can be used in conjunction with tap water to clean both surface pesticides and harmful microorganisms off of produce. E. Coli and other dangerous pathogens have been found on the surface of fruits and vegetables and there have been documented cases of people getting sick due to these nasty pathogens.

In a 2003 study published by the University of Florida, a vinegar mixture containing 10% vinegar was shown to be an effective wash that reduced both bacteria and viruses by more than 90% (32). A study done by the Connecticut Agricultural Experiment Station in 2000 found rinsing produce under tap water to be an effective means of reducing pesticides (33).

Washing produce using a combination of vinegar and tap water appears to be an effective means of reducing both microbial contaminants and pesticide residue. It won't get rid of any pesticides that have leached into the flesh of the produce, but will at least get rid of much of the surface residue.

A solution of ½ cup vinegar to 4 ½ cups of water should get the job done. Be careful using this solution on soft fruits or fruits with porous skins, as they can soak up the vinegar and the flavor will suffer as a result.

Coffee Maker Cleaner

It seems like our K-cup brewer is constantly in use, either making morning coffee for the adults in the house or hot chocolate for the kids. Once a month, I run pure apple cider vinegar through the brewer to clean up any mineral deposits in the hoses and nozzles. When I forget to do this, it never fails—the nozzle that fills the cup slowly gets clogged and is eventually reduced to an excruciatingly slow drip.

If you run ACV through your machine, make sure you run a couple empty cycles of clean water through it before using it to brew coffee again. You don't want your next batch of coffee to taste like vinegar. Learn from my mistakes on this one.

Those of you who are still using a coffee pot can use apple cider vinegar to clean it as well. ACV can be used to clean mineral and hard water stains off the glass and is strong enough to get rid of the cooked-on coffee stains you thought were stuck on the pot forever.

Denture Cleaner

Soak your dentures overnight in apple cider vinegar to keep them clean. In the morning, take them out of the vinegar and brush them to remove tartar build-up. Don't forget to rinse the dentures off before you put them in your mouth! A mouthful of vinegar isn't the best way to wake up in the morning.

Deodorize

Here are just a few of the many areas of the house apple cider vinegar can be used to deodorize:

- **Ashtrays.**
- **Baby rooms.**
- **Bathrooms.**
- **Diaper pails.**
- **Fridges.**
- **Garages.**
- **Garbage cans.**
- **Laundry pails.**
- **Laundry rooms.**
- **Lunchboxes.**
- **Rec rooms.**
- **Recycling bins.**
- **Showers and sinks.**
- **Smoking rooms.**

You name it, there's a pretty good chance ACV can be used to get the stink off it. There are a number of ways in which apple cider can be used to get rid of funky smells. The most direct method is to apply apple cider vinegar directly to the surface that smells. This method works great when you can identify the area that stinks, like when a pet has an accident in the house.

Other times, it may be an entire room or area of the house that smells. When this is the case, instead of attempting to coat the entire room in vinegar, place a bowl or a flat tray of vinegar in the room for a day or two. This will usually get rid of any bad smells in the room.

Alternatively, you can make a deodorizing spray by placing a cup of ACV in a water bottle along with 3 cups of water. When bad smells present themselves, spray it in the air in the smelly area and once the smell of vinegar dissipates, the bad smell should be gone with it. If you can't stand the short-lived smell of vinegar, add 5 to 10 drops of your favorite essential oils to the bottle.

Drain Cleaner

Instead of calling a plumber of resorting to dumping caustic chemicals down the drain the next time you're faced with a clogged drain, turn to apple cider vinegar and baking soda to get the job done. You'll save a few bucks and you won't have to worry about the caustic chemicals eating away at the pipes.

Neither baking soda nor apple cider vinegar work well on their own, but when you combine the two you get a bubbling action that can work its way into a clog and help dissolve and dislodge it. Dump a cup of baking soda down the drain first and let it sit for 10 minutes. Once ten minutes have passed, dump a cup of apple cider vinegar down the drain.

Let it sit for 30 minutes. The vinegar and baking soda may bubble up out of the drain. After 30 minutes have passed, pour a pot of boiling hot water down the drain. The heat should finish loosening up the clog and it should dislodge. This is usually enough to get rid of all but the worst of clogs. If it doesn't work the first time, try it a couple more times before resorting to something stronger.

Microwave Cleaner

Microwaves are notoriously hard to clean. Food and grime gets on the walls of the microwave and is cooked onto the walls repeatedly. By the time you get around to cleaning it, the food has bonded to the walls and is all but impossible to scrub off.

To make cleaning easier, place a bowl of apple cider vinegar in the microwave and nuke it until it starts to steam. Let it steam for a minute or two before opening the microwave and scrubbing away the food. The steam will soften everything up and make it much easier to clean.

Keep your face away from the microwave when you open it. The steam is extremely hot and can cause burns.

Mold and Mildew Cleaner

The fact that apple cider vinegar is antifungal makes it a good tool for mold and mildew cleaning and prevention. Combine 2 cups of ACV with a cup of water and spray it on the moldy area. Let it sit for 15 minutes and wipe the area clean with a soft cloth.

This method can be used to clean small growths of mold or mildew, like what you'd find in the wet areas of a bathroom that's kept relatively clean, but shouldn't be used to clean black mold or vast expanses of mold found in walls or under floors where water has leaked for a long period of time. This type of cleaning is best left to the professionals.

Pet Accidents

If you've got pets, there's a pretty good chance they're going to have an accident in the house from time to time. When pet accidents occur, it's time to whip out the apple cider vinegar.

ACV works on pet accidents in a number of ways. It can be used to lift urine stains out of carpet. Spray diluted ACV on the area of the accident and blot it up. Repeat until the stain is gone. It can also be used to get rid of the smell associated with an accident, which can linger long after the accident has been cleaned up.

Another use for ACV is to discourage pets from going to the bathroom in the house when trying to train them. If you've got a pet that has accidents in the house, spray ACV over the area where they're having the accident. They won't be able to smell the scent of previous accidents there and will be less likely to go in the same place. This is especially effective on cats, as they avoid going to the bathroom in areas where they smell the vinegar.

Streak-Free Window Wash

Washing windows is easy. Washing windows and leaving them free of streaks is a lot harder. That is, unless you use apple cider vinegar to wash your windows. Then you'll have no problem.

Regular window cleaners tend to leave streaks. Even the so-called streak-free glass cleaners don't always work as advertised. Add in fibers that fall off of towels during washing and drying and you've got windows that look dirty mere moments after they've been washed.

Apple cider vinegar can be mixed with water and used to wash windows. Mix a cup of vinegar and two cups of water in a spray bottle and spray it on the window. Wipe the window clean with newspaper instead of a soft cloth and you'll be left with windows that are clean and free of streaks. Just be careful not to walk into glass doors. It's easy to forget they're open when they're crystal-clear.

Leather Reconditioner

Old leather can sometimes be brought back to life using a combination of linseed oil and apple cider vinegar. Combine half a cup of vinegar with a cup of linseed oil and mix it together. Apply it to the leather and massage it in. Wipe the residue away with a soft cloth.

This reconditioner can have unpredictable results, so I don't recommend using it on anything of value. It might however be able to give new life to something old that you would otherwise have to throw away.

Tile and Grout Cleaner

Tile and grout can be a real pain to get clean if you wait a long time between cleanings. Stains can set into grout and will become all but impossible to scrub out.

Apple cider vinegar works well as a tile and grout cleaner, both on counters and on tile floors. Always clean the tile first, before the grout, because you'll get the grout dirty while wiping the tiles clean. The all-purpose cleaner from the beginning of this chapter works well as tile cleaner.

You're going to need something a little bit stronger to use on grout. Mix equal parts water and ACV and spray it onto the grout. Let it sit for a minute or two and scrub it away with a grout brush. If this doesn't work, it's time to break out the big guns. Apply baking soda to the grout and spray apple cider vinegar onto it. It'll start to bubble. Scrub the grout with a toothbrush while the cleaner is bubbling.

The ACV and baking soda are only effective as a cleaner while they're bubbling. Once the bubbling is done, the ACV has been rendered ineffective, so only clean small areas at a time when using this method. Apply baking soda to a small section, add ACV to it and scrub away. Rinse and repeat in another section.

When all else fails, you may be able to use fine-grit sandpaper to sand away the top layer of grout until you get down to the clean stuff. This method is destructive and should only be used as a last resort. Use it at your own risk and be wary of the fact you're removing the grout instead of cleaning it when using this method.

Washing Machine and Dryer Cleaner

Maybe it's because they're used to clean clothes, but the washer and dryer are two of the most neglected items in the house when it comes to cleaning. They can get dirty fast, as they're used to clean and dry clothes that are often covered in dirt, grease and grime.

Cleaning the washing machine is easy, as it only requires tossing a cup of vinegar into the machine on an empty wash cycle. Throw an old towel or two into the machine and it'll pretty much clean itself. You'll have to wipe down the nooks and crannies afterward, but it'll require minimal effort. The dryer is more difficult because you're going to have to do the labor yourself. Use the all-purpose ACV spray from the beginning of the chapter and wipe it down.

If your laundry room smells like sewage, it could be due to the p-trap the washing machine hose is draining into. Try pulling the hose up a little to get it out of the bottom of the trap. If that doesn't work, dump a cup of ACV down the trap to see if it gets rid of the smell.

Wood Scratch Remover

Scratches in dark finished wood can be extremely visible if they're deep enough to get down to the raw wood. A couple scratches in a highly-visible area can make good wood furniture look old and uncared for.

You can sometimes get rid of scratches by rubbing the scratched area with a solution of iodine and vinegar. Start with a few tablespoons of vinegar and mix iodine in until the solution is close to the same color as the wood. Dab a bit on a soft cloth and rub it into the scratch.

It can take a bit of experimentation to get the color right. Always start off lighter than you think you should. It's easier to go darker if you need to, but there isn't much you can do if you use too dark of a color short of sanding and refinishing the wood.

Additional Reading

I hope you enjoyed reading this book and found it helpful. If you enjoyed the household uses section of the book, you might find the following book useful:

How to Clean Your Home Naturally

http://www.amazon.com/Natural-Green-Cleaning-Clean-Naturally-ebook/dp/B00H8IUPY8/

Here's a link to a book about probiotic foods that will help you add beneficial bacteria to your diet:

http://www.amazon.com/Paleo-Probiotics-Fermented-Foods-Living-ebook/dp/B00GYI4F08/

Here's a link to another Paleo recipe book. This one teaches you how to make Paleo bread that's free of gluten and is completely natural:

Paleo Bread

Easy and Delicious Gluten-Free Recipes

Aimee Anderson

http://www.amazon.com/Paleo-Bread-Delicious-Gluten-Free-Recipes-ebook/dp/B00HFD2I1E

Works Cited

1. **Jarvis, D.C.** *Folk MedicineL A Vermont Doctor's Guide to Good Health.* s.l. : Holt, Rhinehart and Winston, 1958.

2. *Antihypertensive effects of acetic acid and vinegar on spontaneously hypertensive rats.* **Shino Kondo, Kenji Tayama, Yoshinori Tsukamoto, Katsumi Ikeda, Yukio Yamori.** 2002, Food & Nutrition Science, Vol. 65, pp. 2690 - 2694.

3. *Quercetin Reduces Blood Pressure in Hypertensive Subjects.* **Randi L. Edwards, Tiffany Lyon, Sheldon E. Litwin, Alexander Rabovsky, J. David Symons, Thunder Jalili.** 11, November 2007, The Journal of Nutrition, Vol. 137, pp. 2405 - 2411.

4. *Dietary acetic acid reduces serum cholesterol and triacylglycerols in rats feda cholesterol-rich diet.* **Takashi Fushimi, Kazuhito Suruga, Yoshifumi Oshima, et al.** 5, s.l. : British Journal of Nutrition, 2006, Vol. 95.

5. *Apple cider vinegar attenuates lipid profile in normal and diabetic rats.* **F Shishehbor, A Mansoori, AR Sarkaki, MT Jalali, SM Latifi.** 23, s.l. : Pak J Biol Sci, 2008, Vol. 11.

6. *Dietary intake of alpha-linolenic acid and risk of fatal ischemic heart disease among women.* **FB Hu, MJ Stampfer, JE Manson, et al.** 5, s.l. : Am J Clin Nutr, 1999, Vol. 69, pp. 890 - 897.

7. *Induction of apoptosis in human leukemia cells by naturally fermented sugar cane vinegar (kibizu) of Amami Ohshima Island.* **A Mimura, Y Suzuki, Y Toshima, S Yazaki, T Ohtsuki, S Ui, F Hyodoh.** 1 - 4, 2004, Biofactors, Vol. 22, pp. 93 - 97.

8. *Protective effects of fermented rice vinegar sediment (Kurozu moromimatsu) in a diethylnitrosamine-induced hepatocellular carcinoma animal model.* **Toru Shizuma, Kazuo Ishiwata, Masanobu Nagano, Hidezo Mori, Naoto Fukuyama.** 1, July 2011, Clinical Biochemistry and Nutrition, Vol. 49, pp. 31 - 35.

9. *Kurozu moromimatsu inhibits tumor growth of Lovo cells in a mouse model in vivo.* **N Fukuyama, S Jujo, I Ito, T Shizuma, K Myojin, K Ishiwata, M Nagano, H Nakazawa, H Mori.** 1, January 2007, Nutrition, Vol. 23, pp. 81 - 86.

10. *Cancer Prevention by Phytochemicals.* **H Nishino, M Murakoshi, XY Mou, S Wada, M Masuda, Y Ohsaka, Y Satomi, K Jinno.** 2005, Oncology, Vol. 69, pp. 38 - 40.

11. *Risk factors for oesophageal cancer in Linzhou, China: a case-control study.* **Xibib S, Meilan H, Moller H, Evans HS, Dixin D, Wenjie D, Jianbang L.** 2, Apr - Jun 2003, Asian Pac J Cancer Prev, Vol. 4, pp. 119 - 124.

12. **Benson, Jonathan.** 10 easy, natural remedies for conquering the common cold. *Natural News.* [Online] Sep 26, 2013. [Cited: 1 7, 2014.] http://www.naturalnews.com/042226_common_cold_natur al_remedies_apple_cider_vinegar.html.

13. **Cespedes, Andrea.** Apple Cider Vinegar Detox Diet. *LiveStrong.* [Online] Aug 16, 2013. [Cited: 1 8 , 2014.] http://www.livestrong.com/article/76566-apple-cider-vinegar-detox-diet/.

14. *Vinegar Improves Insulin Sensitivity to a High-Carbohydrate Meal in Subjects With Insulin Resistance or Type 2 Diabetes.* **Carol S. Johnson, Cindy M. Kim, Amanda J. Buller.** 1, s.l. : Diabetes Care, 2004, Vol. 27, pp. 281 - 282.

15. *Vinegar Ingestion at Bedtime Moderates Waking Glucose Concentrations in Adults With Well-Controlled Type 2 Diabetes.* **Carol S. Johnston, Andera M. White.** 11, November 2007, Diabetes Care, Vol. 30.

16. *Effect of Acetic Acid and Vinegar on Blood Glucose and Insulin Responses to Orally Administered Sucrose and Starch.* **Kiyoshi Ebihara, Akira Nakajima.** 1988, Agric. Biol. Chem., pp. 1311 - 1312.

17. *Examination of the antiglycemic properties of vinegar in healthy adults.* **Carol S Johnston, I Steplewska, CA Long, LN Harris, RH Ryals.** 1, s.l. : Ann. Nutr. Metab., Vol. 56.

18. *Therapeutic effect of daily vinegar ingestion for individuals at risk for type 2 diabetes.* **Carol S Johnston, S Quagliano, S Loeb.** 1079.56, s.l. : FASEB Journal , Vol. 27.

19. **Yanjun.** Appealing health benefits of apple cider vinegar. *Natural News.* [Online] Aug 5, 2013. [Cited: 1 5, 2014.]

http://www.naturalnews.com/041489_apple_cider_vinegar_health_benefits_natural_medicine.html.

20. **Barody, Theodore A.** *Alkalize or Die.* 1991.

21. **Young, Dr. Robert O.** *The pH Miracle.* 2003.

22. **Guide, Editors of Consumer.** Home Remedies for Gout. *Discovery Fit and Health.* [Online] [Cited: 1 9, 2014.] http://health.howstuffworks.com/wellness/natural-medicine/home-remedies/home-remedies-for-gout1.htm.

23. **Alexander, Rhonda.** Is Apple Cider Vinegar a Probiotic? *LiveStrong.* [Online] Dec. 18, 2013. http://www.livestrong.com/article/508833-is-apple-cider-vinegar-a-probiotic/.

24. **Axe, Dr. Josh.** Top 10 Probiotics. *DrAxe.com.* [Online] Mar. 20, 2011. [Cited: 1 2, 2014.] http://www.draxe.com/top-10-probiotics/.

25. **Wilder, Bee.** How to Overcome Candida Naturally. *Food Matters.* [Online] [Cited: 1 9, 2014.] http://foodmatters.tv/articles-1/how-to-overcome-candida-naturally.

26. *The effects of isomaltulose, isomalt, and isomaltulose-based oligomers on mineral absorption and retention.* **Kashimura J, Kimura M, Itokawa Y.** 3, Sep 1996, Biol Trace Elem Res, Vol. 54, pp. 239 - 250.

27. *Enhancing effect of dietary vinegar on the intestinal absorption of calcium in ovariectomized rats.* **Kishi M, Fukaya M, Tsukamoto Y, Nagasawa T, Takehana K, Nishizawa N.** 5, May 1999, Biosci Biotechnol Biochem, Vol. 63, pp. 905 - 910.

28. *Acetic Acid Upregulates the Expression of Genes for Fatty Acid Oxidation Enzymes in Liver To Suppress Body Fat Accumulation.* **Tomoo Kondo, Mikiya Kishi, Takashi Fushimi, Takayuki Kaga.** 13, s.l. : J. Agric. Food Chem., 2009, Vol. 57.

29. *Vinegar Intake Reduces Body Weight, Body Fat Mass, and Serum Triglyceride Levels in Obese Japanese Subjects.* **Tomoo Kondo, et al.** 8, s.l. : Biosci. Biotechnol. Biochem., 2009, Vol. 73, pp. 1837 - 1843.

30. *Vinegar supplementation lowers glucose and insulin responses and increases satiety after a bread meal in healthy subjects.* **Ostman E, Granfeldt Y, Persson L, et al.** s.l. : European Journal of Clinical Nutrition, 2005, Vol. 59, pp. 983-988.

31. *Changes in anthropometric measurements, body composition, blood pressure, lipid profile, and testosterone in patients participating in a low-energy dietary intervention.* **Mary Ballietta, Jeanmarie R. Burkeb.** 1, March 2013, J Chiropr Med, Vol. 12, pp. 3 - 14.

32. *Reduction of poliovirus 1, bacteriophages, Salmonella montevideo, and Escherichia coli O157:H7 on strawberries by physical and disinfectant washes.* **Lukasik J, Bradley ML, Scott TM, Dea M, Koo A, Hsu WY, Bartz JA, Farrah SR.** 2003.

33. **O'Connor, Anahad.** The Claim: A Soap-and-Water Rinse Gets Produce Cleanest. *NY Times.* [Online] Oct 4, 2010. [Cited: 1 7, 2014.] http://www.nytimes.com/2010/10/05/health/05real.html?_r =0.

Made in the USA
Columbia, SC
10 November 2022